Towards Effective Teaching Methods in EFL Listening for Intermediate Learners

I would like to dedicate this book
to Eleanor Ueda, my only daughter,
as a token of my love.

Towards Effective Teaching Methods in EFL Listening for Intermediate Learners

Marisa Ueda

KEISUISHA
2015

Note on author
Marisa Ueda is currently an associate professor at Ritsumeikan University in Japan.
My research interests include listening in EFL.
2011〜2015 Osaka University/Japan (PhD in Language and Culture)
1990〜1991 University of Reading/UK (MA in Applied Linguistics)
1989〜1990 University of East Anglia/UK (Diploma in TEFL)

Copyright © 2015 Marisa Ueda
Printed in Japan

ALL RIGHT RESERVED. No part of this work may be reproduced, redistributed, or used in any form or by any means without prior written permission of the publisher and copy-right owner.

Published by KEISUISHA co., ltd.
1-4 Komachi Naka-ku Hiroshima 730-0041 Japan

ISBN978-4-86327-300-9 C3082

要　旨

　本書は、日本人英語学習者の中でも特に中位層を対象に、効果的なリスニング指導法について論じている。本書の特徴は、大きく 4 つに分類される。1 つ目は、日本人英語学習者の中で一番対象者数が多い中位層に特化した点である。2 つ目は、学習者のリスニング能力に応じて、最適の学習方法を提案していることである。3 つ目は、実験前後の実験協力者のリスニング能力測定及び実験協力者の分類に、標準テストを用いた点である。4 つ目は、リスニング能力向上には、メタ認知における問題解決能力の向上が重要であるということを明らかにしたことである。

　　大学生に中学や高校でリスニングに関して、どのような指導を受けてきたのかを尋ねてみると「注意して聞きなさい。」「わかるまで何回も聞きなさい。」という回答がほぼ全てである。これは、1970 代と全く同じ指導法である。現在までの約 40 年以上、変化が無いこと自体が問題ではなく、その指導法で、日本人英語学習者の多くが未だにリスニングを不得手としていることが問題なのである。「聞いただけではわからないが、見たら（読んだら）わかる。」という学習者は非常に多い。旧態依然としたリスニング指導を、もっと効果的にすることが強く望まれる。

　　第 1 章では、研究目的、本書の構成、本研究で用いられる語句の定義、コミュニケーションにおけるリスニングの占める割合を述べている。本書では、中位層学習者 (TOEIC®のリスニング•テスト 495 点満点中、166〜330 点の学習者)を対象としているが、理由は一番人数が多いからである。2011 年の TOEIC®公式データによると、日本人全受験者の 68.1%がリスニングにおいて中位層である。この現象は 2010 年、2012 年も同じであった。英語学習者の大半がリスニングにおいて中位層であるという現象は、日本を含むアジアや南米の多くの国にも共通している。中位層を対象とした、学習者の能力に合わせた効果的なリスニング指導法を、実証的研究により導きだすことができれば、日本のみならずアジアや南米諸国の英語学習者にも有益である可能性を示している。

第 2 章では、本研究の基礎となっている 2 つの理論やリスニング・ストラテジーについての先行研究で明らかになっていることや論争が継続していること、その原因のいくつかを論じている。認知科学の分野において Schneider and Shiffrin (1977) は、人間の情報処理には 2 段階 (制限過程と自動過程) あると述べている。前者は意識しなければ遂行できない行動で、後者はそれを繰り返し行うことで、徐々に意識しなくてもできるようになってくる行動である。また、応用言語学の分野では Anderson (2010) が、言語学習における 3 段階 (perception, parsing, utilisation) からなる認知心理学理論を唱えている。この理論を用いれば、どのレベルで学習者が理解できなくなったかをピンポイントで指摘することが可能である。先行研究で明らかになっていることは、主に 3 つで、上位層学習者はトップ・ダウンとボトム・アップの両方を用いているということ、下位層学習者は主にボトム・アップを用いているということ、両者の決定的な相違は、上位層学習者が複数のメタ認知ストラテジー (planning, monitoring, evaluation) を用いているということである。論争が継続している点は、上位層学習者が用いているリスニング・ストラテジーを下位層学習者に指導すれば、リスニング能力が向上するのではないか、ということであり、賛成派と懐疑派に分裂している。その原因の一つとして、多くの先行研究において標準テスト (国際的に有名であり入手が容易、なおかつ他のテストと互換性があるテスト) が使われていないことや、実験協力者がどのように選別・分類されたのかが明確にされていないことが考えられる。標準テストが用いられていないことにより、多くの先行研究結果を他の研究結果と科学的且つ客観的に比較することができないのである。そこで、本書では標準テストとして TOEIC® のリスニング・テストを用い、3 分割 (0〜165, 166〜330, 331〜495) した上で、166〜330 点の学習者を中位層学習者として実験協力者とした。TOEIC® は以下の様に、複数の標準テストに大まかではあるが換算可能である。

TOEFL®	TOEFL®iBT	IELTS	Cambridge	TOEIC®	EIKEN
677	120	9.0	CPE	990	
650	115	7.5–8.5		890	
600	100	6.0–7.0	CAE	660–810	Grade 1
550	80				
500	61	5.5	FCE	590	Grade Pre-1
470	52	5.0		450–520	
		4.5			
450	45	3.5–4.0	PET	310–380	Grade Pre-2 to Grade 2
		2.5–3.0	KET	220	Grade 3
		1.0–2.0	Young Learners		Grade 4 to 5

　第3章では、第1実験としてディクテーション訓練とリスニング•ストラテジー訓練の実証研究手法や結果を論じている。前者は上記2つの理論に基づいた訓練で、音素や語句の音声による知覚•反復学習である。後者は、複数のメタ認知ストラテジーの理論と実践学習である。実験期間は15週間、初回講義でTOEIC®のリスニング•テストで108名の実験協力者を選別し、3群 (統制群10名、ディクテーション訓練群52名、リスニング•ストラテジー訓練群46名) に分類した。第2〜14週の13週間毎週1回、統制群には通常講義のみ、ディクテーション訓練群には、弱音や連結などを含むディクテーション訓練を、リスニング•ストラテジー訓練群には複数のリスニング•ストラテジーの理論と実践を各群90分の通常講義内に30分行った。最終週である15週目にTOEIC®のリスニング•テストを実施し、第1週のデータと比較して各訓練の効果を分析した。分析手法には、分散分析や多重比較 (ライアン法)、効果量、散布図を用いた。その結果、ディクテーション訓練とリスニング•ストラテジー訓練の両方に有意差が得られた。また、中位層学習者をさらに下•中位層学習者 (第1週のTOEIC®のリスニング•テストで166〜249点の学習者) と上•中位層学習者 (第1週のTOEIC®のリスニング•テストで250〜330点の学習者) とに分けて分析した結果、前者には特にディクテーション訓練に有意差が得られた。この結果は、人間の情報処理や言語学習には下から積み上げるように、段階を経て向上していくという上記2つの理論と整合する。

第4章では、第2実験として第3章で有意差が得られた2つの訓練を複合した複合訓練の実証研究手法や結果を論じている。実験期間や実験協力者の選別・分類、実験結果の分析手法は第1実験と同様である。実験協力者は57名で、統制群 (28名) には通常講義のみ、複合訓練群 (29名) には第1実験で実施した両訓練を90分の通常講義内にそれぞれ30分ずつ合計60分行った。第1実験では2つの訓練に有意差が得られたが、得点が下がった実験協力者もいた。そこで、第2実験では、MALQというリスニングにおけるメタ認知に関するアンケートという分析要素を増やし、第1及び15週に実施した。結果、複合訓練に有意差は得られなかった。個々に指導された場合、有意差が得られる指導法であっても、複合された場合、中位層には処理しきれない膨大な情報量となってしまい、効果がなかったと推測される。この結果は、上記2つの理論と整合する。また、MALQの分析結果から、複合訓練群の点数が上がった上位11名の実験協力者に共通することは、計画/評価能力と問題解決能力の向上であった。具体的には、聞く前にどのように聞くのか計画を立てたり、聞いた後に次回からはどのようにして聞くべきであるかを内省したり、分からないところがあっても、言語能力のみならず他の認知能力を活用し、諦めずに聞き続け理解しようとする態度や今までの理解が間違いであると判断した時は、直ぐに考えを切り替えるといった能力の向上である。

　第5章では、第3実験として第1実験の瑕疵2点 (統制群の実験協力者数が10名と少なかったことやMALQを用いていなかったこと。) を補うための実証研究手法や結果を論じている。実験期間や実験協力者の選別・分類、実験結果の分析手法は第1実験と同様であり、MALQを第1及び15週に実施した。実験協力者は94名で、統制群 (23名)、ディクテーション訓練群 (34名)、リスニング・ストラテジー訓練群 (37名)に分類した。結果、第1実験と同様にディクテーション訓練とリスニング・ストラテジー訓練の両方に有意差が得られた。特に上・中位層学習者にはリスニング・ストラテジー訓練に有意差が得られた。この結果は、第1・2実験同様、上記2つの理論と整合する。さらに、MALQの分析結果から、特別なリスニングの訓練を受けない場合やディクテーション訓練ではメタ認知ストラテジーは向上しないことも明らかになった。リスニング・ストラテジー訓練は、翻訳をせずに聞く能力や聞く前にどのように聞くかの計画を立てたり、聞いた

Japanese Abstract

後に次回からはどのようにして聞くべきであるかを内省したり、分からないところがあっても、言語能力のみならず他の認知能力を活用し、諦めずに聞き続け理解しようとする態度の向上に効果があることが判明した。点数が上がったリスニング・ストラテジー訓練群の上位12名の実験協力者に共通することは、第2実験同様、問題解決能力の向上であった。具体的には、分からないところがあっても、言語能力のみならず他の認知能力を活用し、諦めずに聞き続け理解しようとする態度や今までの理解が間違いであると判断した時は、直ぐに考えを切り替えるといった能力の向上である。

　第6章では、3つの実験結果をまとめるとともに、研究結果を元にした学習者の習熟度に応じた診断的で具体的なリスニング指導法を述べた。また、今後の研究の指針として次の3点を述べた。

(1) アジアや南アメリカの国での研究：中位層学習者が大半を占めるこれらの国で、本書と同様の研究を行った場合、同様の効果や結果が得られるだろうか。理論的には、本研究と同様の結果が得られる筈であるが、文化や習慣などの違いという要因もあり、リスニング研究へのさらなる貢献のために研究結果を検証する必要がある。

(2) 統制群無しでの研究：1週間に一度30分通常講義の中で、先にディクテーション訓練を6週間、その後リスニング・ストラテジー訓練を同期間指導する群と、先にリスニング・ストラテジー訓練を6週間、その後ディクテーション訓練を同期間指導する群の2群に分けて実験を行った場合、どのような効果や結果が得られるだろうか。実証的な研究であっても、統制群を持たない新しいスタイルで検証することは可能である。

(3) 教室で導入する指導法の効果について：統計的に有意であると出た指導法であっても他の指導者が同じ方法を用いて効果を上げるかどうかは別の問題である。効果を上げるためには、適切な運用が欠かせず、適切な運用は指導者が常に学生の反応や理解度といった現場を見ながら判断していくことが重要で、方法と運用は常にセットになっていることを指導者は強く認識する必要がある。最終的には、様々な条件や制約を考えながら如何に本研究結果を教育の現場に還元するかを考えていかねばならない。

Abstract

This study investigates effective teaching methods in English as a foreign language (EFL) listening specifically for intermediate learners based on the theories of Schneider and Shiffrin (1977) and Anderson (1980). Both theories claim that there are gradual steps in human information processing and language learning, respectively. The present study is unique for several reasons. Firstly, it focuses on intermediate learners in EFL listening. In this study, the term 'intermediate' refers to those with the Test of English for International Communication® (TOEIC®) listening scores between 166 and 330. In general, the maximum attainable TOEIC® listening score is 495, which is sub-divided into three score ranges, i.e. low (0–165), intermediate (166–330) and high (331–495). Previous listening strategy studies have primarily focussed on listeners at two competency levels to reveal how skilled listeners outperform their less-skilled counterparts. Thus, the present study fills the gap by examining this particular level.

Second, a standardised test is employed to define the proficiency level of the participants *before* the studies and to measure the effects of different teaching methods both *before* and *after* the studies. In this study, a standardised test is defined as any language proficiency test that is reliable, international, popular, relatively easy to access and capable of being compared/converted to other tests. Some previous studies about EFL/ESL listening strategies have shown that, for less-skilled learners, it is effective to teach the listening strategies that are employed by skilled listeners (Rubin, 1994; Cross, 2009; Graham, Santos and Vanderplank, 2011), whereas other studies question such an approach (Field, 2008; Lynch, 2009). One of the reasons for such a debate is mainly due to the lack of using a standardised test, which diminishes the overall generalisability of the

Abstract

findings. For, researchers' classifications of learners as skilled- or less-skilled listeners vary significantly across studies, and without the use of a standardised test, those categorised as skilled-listeners in one study might be grouped as intermediate in another, whilst those categorised as intermediate in one study might be classified as less-skilled listeners in another. Hence, the present study is unique since it utilises a standardised test to focus on intermediate learners within the framework of EFL listening strategies.

Third, the present study provides diagnostic instructions based on the proficiency level of the participants, the results of this study and Anderson's (2010) theory. For decades, instructors have merely provided students with an opportunity to listen. However, instruction concerning *how* to listen was rarely taught. Consequently, by interviewing the participants and analysing their errors, it is possible to pinpoint where comprehension breaks down, which can be specifically helpful for instructors regarding effective teaching methods for students.

The following hypotheses are tested in this study:

H-1 For intermediate listeners, dictation training is more effective than listening strategy training.

H-2 For low-intermediate listeners, dictation training is more effective.

H-3 For intermediate listeners, the combined training of dictation and listening strategy is not effective for improving EFL listening comprehension.

H-4 For intermediate listeners, the combined training of dictation and listening strategy is not significantly effective for improving metacognitive skills in EFL listening.

H-5 For intermediate listeners, both dictation training and listening strategy training are effective with significance.

H-6 For upper-intermediate listeners, listening strategy training is more effective.

H-7   Intermediate listeners with listening strategy training show a greater change in their metacognitive skills.

Three experimental studies were conducted: Studies I, II and III. The participants consisted of 259 Japanese university students at the intermediate level in EFL listening. Study I involved 108 participants to examine Hypotheses 1 and 2. The results reveal that dictation training is significantly more effective for intermediate listeners than listening strategy training, and that dictation training is significantly more effective for low-intermediate listeners. Study II comprised 57 participants to examine Hypotheses 3 and 4. The results reveal that, for intermediate listeners, the combined training of dictation and listening strategy is not effective for improving EFL listening comprehension and metacognitive skills in EFL listening. In addition, intermediate listeners do not improve their metacognitive skills in EFL listening without special listening training. Study III was conducted with 94 participants to examine Hypotheses 5, 6 and 7. The results indicate five aspects:

1) Both dictation training and listening strategy training are significantly effective for intermediate listeners.
2) Listening strategy training is significantly effective, especially for upper-intermediate listeners.
3) Listening strategy training is effective for intermediate listeners to improve some metacognitive skills in EFL listening such as mental translation, planning/evaluation and problem solving.
4) Dictation training is not effective for intermediate to improve metacognitive skills in EFL listening.
5) The improvement of planning/evaluation and problem solving in metacognitive skills is vital for becoming an advanced listener in EFL listening.

All these results are in agreement with the theories of Schneider and Shiffrin (1977) and Anderson (1980).

Acknowledgements

This book could not have been completed without the help of many people. First, I would like to express my utmost gratitude to Professor Isao Ueda at Osaka University, the chair of my dissertation committee. He helped me and provided valuable suggestions and constructive advice for which I never lost the right directions in the past four years. His insightful suggestions and incisive advice were literally the shining light in a dark cave for me.

My genuine gratitude also goes to Associate Professor Andrew Murakami-Smith, the vice chair of my dissertation committee at Osaka University. He always attended my presentations patiently despite my research field is not an exact match of his.

I would like to state my sincere gratitude to Professor Nobuyuki Hino, the vice chair of my dissertation committee at Osaka University. In 2012, I took his extremely high quality lectures about presentations in English. What most inspired me is his new research plan without a control group.

My genuine gratitude also goes to Professor Hisashi Iwane and Dr Yasuhiro Imao at Osaka University. Professor Iwane was tremendously compassionate to teach me many helpful statistical skills whenever I was distressed. Dr Imao also encouraged and helped me about Effect Size—a new measurement in statistics. My dissertation significantly improved with their indomitable support.

I would also like to express my sincere gratitude to Professor Tomoko Okita at Osaka University. Although I was the only student, she patiently taught me pragmatics in 2012. The content of her class is priceless since it is firmly related with one of the listening strategies (inference) and the highest level (utilisation) in Anderson's cognitive psychology theory. My dissertation was considerably enhanced because of her enthusiastic instruction.

My special thanks go to Professor Hiroki Iwai at Osaka University. His unique and meaningful lectures inspired me how to motivate learners skilfully.

My sincere gratitude goes to Professor Masato Hayashi at Ritsumeikan University. He provided a beam of light when I had almost given up pursuing a Ph.D. degree in 2010. This was an opportunity of a lifetime for me. I cannot thank him enough for this.

I would like to express my gratitude to former Professor Mikihiko Sugimori at Ritsumeikan University. He greatly inspired and encouraged me to research listening comprehension in EFL when I came back to Japan from England.

My heartfelt thanks go to Dr Sarah Dodd in Lancaster in England for her continuous and warm encouragement. She is my best friend and the only one that I could confess that I was reading for a Ph.D. degree.

I wish also to thank Ms Tokiko Kimura, Keisuisha Publishing Co., Ltd. For her generous advices and hearty support in publishing this book. Then I would like to acknowledge gratefully the budget provided by Ritsumeikan University: Programme for Promotion of Academic Publication.

Finally, my gratefulness goes to my daughter Eleanor. She is always my rock and my strength. I was determined to keep it secret even to my parents and my own daughter that I began to pursue my Ph.D. degree until the day I received it. Eleanor was only 10 when I started my Ph.D. She has always been patient whilst I was working as a full-time lecturer and as a full-time postgraduate student in the past four years. Hereafter, I do look forward to spending much more time with her.

Many people supported me in various ways. Without even one person, this book could not have been completed. To these people, I owe the success of this dissertation. As for any shortcomings, these are mine.

Table of Contents

Japanese Abstract i
Abstract vi
Acknowledgements ix
Table of Contents xi

Chapter 1: Introduction 1
  1.1 Background of the Study 1
      1.1.1 Teaching of EFL listening in Japan during the late 1970s 1
      1.1.2 Ratio of listening in communication 2
  1.2 Definitions of Terms 3
  1.3 Purpose 4
  1.4 Overview of the Chapters 10

Chapter 2: Literature Review 12
  2.1 What has Become Clear 12
      2.1.1 Controlled and automatic human information processing .. 12
      2.1.2 Cognitive psychology theory 13
      2.1.3 Mental process in listening comprehension and cognitive
           psychology theory 18
      2.1.4 Differences in the listening comprehension strategies by
           proficiency levels 18
  2.2 Previous Research Arguments 27
      2.2.1 Teachability and effectiveness of explicit strategies
           instruction 27
      2.2.2 Lack of a standardised test to measure participants'
           proficiency and compare results 29
      2.2.3 Lack of studies about the intermediate level 34

Chapter 3: Study I - Dictation Training and Listening Strategy Training 38
   3.1 Hypotheses 38
   3.2 Method 40
      3.2.1 Participants 40
      3.2.2 Materials 42
      3.2.3 Procedure 43
   3.3 Results 49
   3.4 Discussion 58
      3.4.1 Discussion about the pre- and post-data for the CG, DTG and LSTG 58
      3.4.2 Discussion about the two-way ANOVA, multiple comparison, effect size and scatter plot 59
      3.4.3 Discussion about the DTG and LSTG participants whose scores increased in Week 15 62
      3.4.4 Discussion about the DTG and LSTG participants whose scores decreased in Week 15 64
   3.5 Summary 65

Chapter 4: Study II - Combined Training with the MALQ 67
   4.1 Hypotheses 67
   4.2 Method 68
      4.2.1 Participants 68
      4.2.2 Materials 69
      4.2.3 Procedure 71
   4.3 Results 72
   4.4 Discussion 82
      4.4.1 Discussion about the pre- and post-data for the CG and D+LSTG 82
      4.4.2 Discussion about the two-way ANOVA, effect size and scatter plot 83

  4.4.3 Discussion about the D+LSTG participants whose scores increased and decreased in Week 15 84
  4.4.4 Discussion about the MALQ 86
 4.5 Summary 94

Chapter 5: Study III - Dictation Training and Listening Strategy Training with the MALQ 97
 5.1 Hypotheses 97
 5.2 Method 98
  5.2.1 Participants 98
  5.2.2 Materials 100
  5.2.3 Procedure 100
 5.3 Results 101
 5.4 Discussion 118
  5.4.1 Discussion about the pre- and post-data for the CG, DTG and LSTG 119
  5.4.2 Discussion about the two-way ANOVA, multiple comparison, effect size and scatter plot 120
  5.4.3 Discussion about the DTG and LSTG participants whose scores increased in Week 15 121
  5.4.4 Discussion about the DTG and LSTG participants whose scores decreased in Week 15 125
  5.4.5 Discussion about the MALQ 127
 5.5 Summary 136

Chapter 6: Summary, Implications and Suggestions 139
 6.1 Overview of the Studies 139
 6.2 Overview of the Findings 141
 6.3 Implications of the Study 142
 6.4 Suggestions for Future Research 146

References 149

Appendix A	Schedule of Study I	159
Appendix B	Materials for Dictation Training Group	161
Appendix C	Materials for Listening Strategies Training Group	186
Appendix D	Raw data of Study I	203
Appendix E	Schedule of Study II	204
Appendix F	The MALQ	206
Appendix G	Raw data of Study II	208
Appendix H	Schedule of Study III	209
Appendix I	Raw data of Study III	211

Chapter 1: Introduction

1.1 Background of the Study
1.1.1 Teaching of English as a foreign language listening in Japan during the late 1970s

For more than four decades, English as a foreign language (EFL) listening classes in Japan have remained relatively unchanged. For example, during the late 1970s, when I was a junior high school student, our English teacher frequently instructed us to 'listen carefully' and 'listen many times'. However, no matter how carefully or how many times we listened, occasionally, it was still difficult to comprehend the texts. In addition, the teacher neglected to indicate where and why our comprehension was incorrect or what should be the subsequent step. Instead, the teacher simply presented the answers along with the audio script. Currently, I teach EFL listening classes at a university in Japan, and at the beginning of every academic year, I ask my students whether they understand the concepts of scanning and skimming, which are basic listening strategies; merely one or two students in each class are aware of such strategies. Thus, it is apparent that the situation has remained unchanged for nearly 40 years; that is, learners are tested and exposed to listening but not taught 'how to listen'. According to Mendelsohn (1995, pp. 132–133), second/foreign language teachers have limited confidence on how to teach their students to listen.

Moreover, if learners are taught listening strategies or 'how to listen', then would their listening comprehension in EFL improve? Before seeking an answer to this question, it is necessary to first focus on the importance of listening in communication.

1.1.2 Ratio of listening in communication

It has long been a common misunderstanding that speaking skill in EFL is a prominent skill in communication. In fact, the majority of the students in my classes seem to be much more interested in speaking than in listening. Richards (2005, ix) claims that listening is still somewhat neglected in second language acquisition research, but it plays a more central role in language teaching.

Previous studies report that listening is a vital aspect of communication. For example, Rivers (1984) reports that adults spend 40%–50% of their communication time listening, 25%–30% speaking, 11%–16% reading and 9% writing (Figure 1.1).

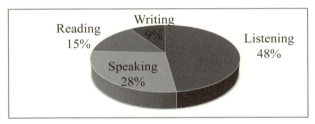

Figure 1.1 **Total time devoted to communication (Rivers (1984))**

Similarly, Yorio (1992) describes listening comprehension as an extremely important skill for adults because they spend approximately half of their communication time in listening (Figure 1.2).

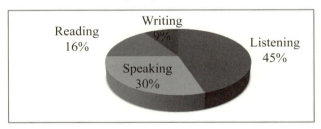

Figure 1.2 **Total time devoted to communication (Yorio (1992))**

Rubin and Rubin (1995, p. 7) make an even stronger claim that listening is a critical aspect of communication and that 50% of a person's time is spent listening (Figure 1.3).

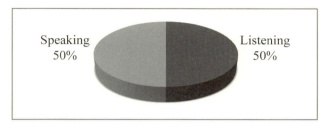

Figure 1.3   Total time devoted to communication (Rubin and Rubin (1995))

These aforementioned studies elucidate that listening actually has a much greater share of communication and language comprehension than we possibly think. Conversely, it is true that experimental research in EFL listening is much less than that in EFL reading. According to Anderson (2010, p. 358), researchers' choice between written or spoken material is determined by what is experimentally easier to conduct. Although listening shares a much greater portion than any other communication skill, many aspects of EFL listening remain rather unclear. As previously stated, if learners are taught 'how to listen' or listening strategies, would their listening comprehension in EFL improve? Some studies respond with a 'yes' (Rubin, 1994; Cross, 2009; Graham, Santos and Vanderplank, 2011), whereas others are 'sceptical' (Field, 2008; Lynch, 2009).

1.2 Definitions of Terms

The terms used in this study are defined as follows:

Bottom-up processing:

This refers to an action or procedure that begins by gathering the smallest items and combining them into larger holistic ideas (Lynch and Mendelsohn, 2002).

Top-down processing:
This refers to an action or procedure that begins with broad global notions and moves towards smaller individual units (Lynch and Mendelsohn, 2002).

Listening:
This refers to understanding spoken English in a non-collaborative situation and interpreting a speaker's utterances.

Dictation:
In this dissertation, dictation refers to the act of listening to one sentence or a very short passage in English and writing down what has been heard. The use of knowledge of grammar or background context is minimal, since the length of one sentence or a passage is very short. Listeners primarily utilise acoustic information to interpret the spoken words and phrases.

Listening strategy/strategies:
This term represents listeners' conscious intention to manage incoming oral speech, especially when listeners know that they must compensate for incomplete input or partial understanding (Rost, 2002, p. 236).

Intermediate listeners:
This term refers to those with the Test of English for International Communication® (TOEIC®) listening scores between 166 and 330. The maximum attainable TOEIC® listening score is 495, and it is sub-divided into three score ranges, i.e. low (0–165), intermediate (166–330) and high (331–495).

1.3 Purpose

This study investigates the effects of three different teaching methods (i.e. dictation training, listening strategy training and combined training of dictation and listening strategy) on intermediate learners in Japan within the framework of applied linguistics and cognitive psychology by using a standardised test. For this study, the listening parts of the TOEIC® are used as the standardised test since it is international, popular, relatively easy to access and capable of being compared/converted to other tests.

This study focuses on intermediate learners for three reasons. First, studies on the listening strategies of intermediate EFL learners are insufficient. Previous listening strategy studies have primarily focussed on listeners at two competency levels to reveal how skilled listeners outperform their less-skilled counterparts (DeFilippis, 1980; Murphy, 1987; O'Malley, Chamot and Küpper, 1989; Rost and Ross, 1991; Moreira, 1996; Vandergrift, 1997; Goh, 2000; Shirono, 2003; Ueda, 2005; Graham, Santos and Vanderplank, 2008; Vandergrift and Tafaghodtari, 2010). However, unlike advanced listeners, intermediate listeners may not have attained the skill level to effectively apply the results of these studies, which do not specifically focus on intermediate listeners. Thus, studies that directly focus on effective instructional strategies for intermediate listeners are necessary.

Second, the majority of EFL learners in Japan are at the intermediate level, which I have realised through personal experience. For instance, since 2011 at the beginning of every academic year, I administer the listening parts of the TOEIC® to my students in order to survey their level of listening comprehension. The results show that the population of intermediate learners comprised 91% (148 of 163 students) in 2011, 90% (116 of 129 students) in 2012, 99% (115 of 116 students) in 2013 and 99% (115 of 116 students) in 2014 (Figure 1.4). From a macro perspective, I also examined the population of intermediate learners in the TOEIC® official report. Figure 1.5 shows that this phenomenon occurs not only at the university I teach at but also at the majority of universities in Japan. For example, in 2011, the average TOEIC® listening score of university students in Japan was 304.

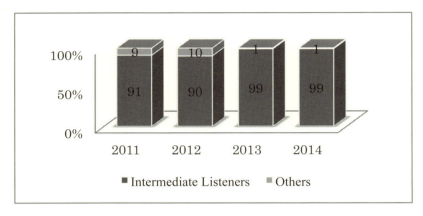

Figure 1.4 Proportions of intermediate listeners in the author's classes from 2011 to 2014

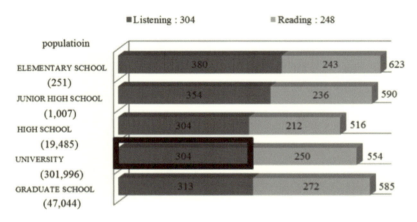

Figure 1.5 Average score of Japanese university students on the listening parts of the TOEIC® in 2011

Introduction

In addition, this phenomenon is observed not only amongst Japanese university students but also amongst all Japanese learners of English, as evidenced in Figure 1.6. A total of 68.1% of test takers were categorised as intermediate learners on the listening section.

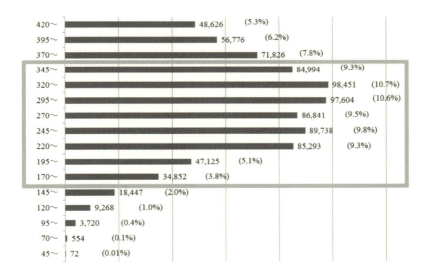

Figure 1.6 Score ranges of the listening parts of the TOEIC® in Japan in 2011

This phenomenon regarding the majority of the Japanese learners of English being at the intermediate level was not an isolated occurrence in 2011. As shown in Figure 1.7, the average TOEIC® listening scores in 2010, 2011 and 2012 were 258, 257 and 256, respectively, each of which falls within the 166–330 range, or the intermediate level.

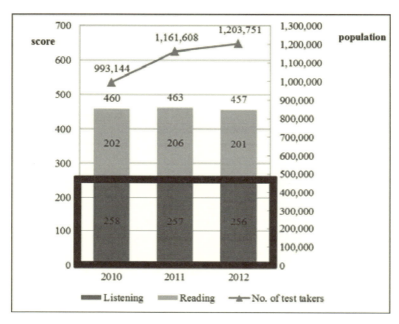

Figure 1.7 Average scores of Japanese learners of English on the listening parts of the TOEIC® in 2010, 2011 and 2012

Third, the characteristic that the majority of English learners are categorised as intermediate in listening is not only observed in Japan but also in other countries throughout Asia and South America. According to the TOEIC® worldwide report of 2012, the average listening scores of Korea, Turkey, Taiwan, Japan, Hong Kong, Thailand, Macao, Vietnam, Indonesia, Columbia, Peru, Brazil, Mexico, Chile and Ecuador fall in the intermediate level (Table 1.1 and Figure 1.8).

Introduction

Table 1.1   Excerpt of Average Listening Scores on the TOEIC® in Asia and South America in 2011

Asia		South America	
Korea	342	Columbia	317
Turkey	306	Peru	311
Taiwan	295	Brazil	308
Japan	284	Mexico	308
Hong Kong	281	Chile	306
Thailand	280	Ecuador	282
Macao	266		
Vietnam	245		
Indonesia	195		

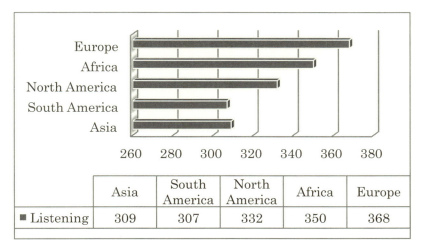

	Asia	South America	North America	Africa	Europe
■ Listening	309	307	332	350	368

Figure 1.8   Average scores of the listening parts of the TOEIC® per region in 2012

9

Therefore, the results of this study can be highly practical and beneficial for many intermediate learners of English not only in Japan but also in Asia and South America. Based on the aforementioned reasons, this study explores effective teaching methods in EFL listening for intermediate learners primarily in Asia and South America.

1.4 Overview of the Chapters

This book consists of six chapters. Following this introductory chapter, Chapter 2 introduces two fundamental theories, reviews previous studies on EFL and English as a second language (ESL) listening strategies and describes what has been clarified and argued in the field of EFL/ESL listening strategies. This is followed by the justification for this study.

In Chapter 3, the details of Study I (conducted from April to July 2012) are described along with the research hypotheses. In Study I, the participants were selected in Week 1; thereafter, they were divided into two groups and required to perform two different types of training (i.e. dictation training and listening strategy training), respectively in their usual weekly class of 90 minutes for 13 weeks. This was followed by the listening parts of the TOEIC® in Week 15 to evaluate the effects of such training. The results are discussed based on the data obtained from statistical analyses.

Chapter 4 presents the details of Study II (conducted from April to July 2013) along with the research hypotheses. In Study II, the participants were selected in Week 1; thereafter, they were required to perform a combined training of dictation and listening strategies training in their usual weekly class of 90 minutes for 13 weeks. This was followed by the listening parts of the TOEIC® in Week 15 to observe the effects of the combined training. The participants were also asked to answer the Metacognitive Awareness Listening Questionnaire (MALQ) in Weeks 1 and 15. The results are discussed based on the data obtained from statistical analyses.

Chapter 5 provides the details of Study III (conducted from September 2013 to January 2014) along with the research hypotheses. In Study III, the participants were selected in Week 1; thereafter, they were they were divided into two groups and required to perform two different types of training (i.e. dictation training and listening strategy training), respectively in their usual weekly class for 90 minutes for 13 weeks. This was followed by the listening parts of the TOEIC® in Week 15 to evaluate the effects of such training. The results are discussed based on the data obtained from statistical analyses. The difference between Studies I and III is that in the latter study, the participants were asked to answer the MALQ in Weeks 1 and 15.

Finally, Chapter 6 presents a summary of all the studies and their results. It also states the implications of this study, followed by suggestions for future research within the framework of both applied linguistics and cognitive psychology.

Chapter 2: Literature Review

The purpose of this chapter is twofold. First, it reviews the literature about ESL/EFL listening strategies and presents the research clarifications. Second, it describes the existing and continuing arguments.

2.1 What has Become Clear
2.1.1 Controlled and automatic human information processing

Schneider and Shiffrin (1977) propose that learning includes two types of cognitive processing, i.e. controlled and automatic human information processing. Controlled processing involves a sequence of cognitive activities under active control which draw the conscious attention of the subject. Conversely, automatic processing involves a sequence of cognitive activities that automatically occur without active control and generally without conscious attention. This theory is supported by numerous studies (Lynch, 1998; Goh, 2000; Buck, 2001; Anderson, 2010). Buck (2001) adeptly illustrates both types of processing by comparing them to the scenario of learning to drive a car. In this regard, initially, the entire learning process is controlled, thus requiring conscious attention to every action. After more experience, certain parts of the process become relatively automatic and are performed subconsciously. Eventually, the entire process becomes automatic to the extent that, under normal circumstances, one has the ability to drive a car well and without much thought. Figure 2.1 demonstrates the hierarchical model of controlled and automatic human information processing, following Schneider and Shiffrin (1977).

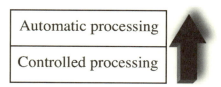

Figure 2.1 Hierarchical model of controlled and automatic human information processing in Schneider and Shiffrin (1977)

Based on this theory, dictation in listening is categorised as controlled processing (bottom-up processing) since it involves phonemic decoding, which requires conscious attention to phonemes, the smallest segments of sound (Ladefoged, 1982). In contrast, from a listening strategy perspective, the identification of individual words is mainly regarded as automatic processing (top-down processing), because it can only be possible after phonemic decoding occurs automatically without active control and conscious attention. Thus, the less automatic an activity becomes, the more time and cognitive energy it requires. In this regard, when learners take more time in phonemic decoding, their overall comprehension suffers. This situation is similar to the idiom of missing the forest for the trees. The following section introduces a theory used in the field of language learning which includes a similar concept.

2.1.2 Cognitive psychology theory

Anderson (2010) claims that language learning involves certain steps and proposes a cognitive framework of language comprehension based on *perception*, *parsing* and *utilisation*. Although these three phases are interrelated, recursive and possibly concurrent, they differ from one another. At the lowest cognitive level of listening, perception is the decoding of acoustic input that involves extracting phonemes from a continuous stream of speech.

With regard to the first stage, Anderson (2010) argues that there are at least two problems in speech perception or recognition, i.e. segmentation and co-articulation. The first problem, segmentation, occurs when the phonemes need to be identified, but unlike printed text, speech is not broken into discrete units. Speech is a continuous stream of sounds with no noticeable word boundaries. Thus, any new learner of English normally experiences this problem. Anderson defines *phonemes* as the minimal units of speech that can result in a difference in the spoken message (p. 51). Words are divided into two categories, i.e. content and function words. Nouns, verbs, adjectives, adverbs and demonstrative pronouns are categorised as content words (Gimson, 1980, p. 256); they convey relevant information unlike function words such as prepositions, conjunctions and determiners. Thus, function words are not generally stressed in listening. Furthermore, the segmentation problem and unstressed words are firmly related. Examples of the segmentation problem include assimilation, contraction, deletion, elision, liaison/linking and reduction (Yoshida, 2002, p. 32).

According to Ladefoged (1982, p. 99), assimilation occurs when one sound is changed into another because of the influence of a neighbouring sound (e.g. 'Red Cross' can be heard as */reg kros/* and 'hot pie' as */hop pai/*).

Contraction is defined as a vowel-less weak form by Knowles (1987, p. 146). Examples of contractions in sentences, especially in rapid speech, include 'going to' which becomes 'gonna', as in 'I'm *gonna* do it tomorrow'; 'got to', which becomes 'gotta', as in 'I've *gotta* go' and 'I would', which becomes 'I'd', as in '*I'd* say so'.

Deletion is the removal of a part of the pronunciation. For example, in rapid speech, 'because' becomes 'cuz', as in 'I'm studying English *cuz* I'm going abroad', and 'them' becomes 'em', as in 'Why don't you go with *em*?'

Rost and Wilson (2013, p. 305) use 'elided' to describe elision, which is defined as the omission of sounds in rapid connected speech. They also state that this is usually the result of one word 'sliding' into another, and the sound omitted is usually an initial or final sound in a word (e.g. 'soft pillow' can be heard as /sof pilow/ and 'old man' as /oul man/).

According to Cutler (2012), liaison is 'a final sound pronounced only when the following word begins with a vowel…it interacts with segmentation of the speech stream' (p. 206). Examples include 'I'll need to thin*k a*bout it', 'The sheep lick*ed u*p the milk' and 'No*t at a*ll'.

Finally, as an example of reduction, which reduces the number of vowels that occur in unaccented syllables (Knowles, 1987, p. 97), Yoshida (2002) introduces a sentence such as 'You dropped your handkerchief' in which the word 'your' is not stressed (p. 32). This phenomenon occurs because the word 'your' is a function word and is unstressed.

The second problem in speech perception involves a phenomenon known as co-articulation (Liberman, 1970). Ladefoged (1982, p. 52) defines co-articulation as the overlapping of adjacent articulations; that is, as the vocal tract is producing one sound, it moves towards the shape for the following phoneme. For example, the sound of /b/ itself and the /b/ in 'bag' are different. Thus, when pronouncing /b/ in 'bag', the vocal tract is already moving towards the next sound /a/. In addition, when pronouncing /a/ in 'bag', the root of our tongue is raised to produce the /g/. These segmentation problems pose complications for any learner of English, since an independent phenomenon of segmentation does not usually occur in a single sentence. Rather multiple phenomena of segmentation might occur in just a single sentence. Moreover, these difficulties exist only in perception, the lowest cognitive level of listening. Anderson (2010, p. 52) describes that speech perception poses information-processing demands that are, in many ways, greater than what is involved in other types of auditory perception.

Many Japanese learners of English encounter these segmentation problems. Ikemura (2003) indicates that the auditory recognition of words is one of the major problems at the speech perception level for Japanese learners of English. This is because reading and writing are generally emphasised at schools in Japan; this is evidenced by the fact that it was only since 2006 when a listening comprehension test was introduced in the national examination of Japanese universities.

Next, the second stage in Anderson's cognitive psychology theory (2010) is parsing. In parsing, words are transformed into a mental representation of the combined meaning of the words. This occurs when a listener segments an utterance according to syntactic structures or meaning cues. According to Anderson (2010), people use the syntactic cues of word order and inflection to interpret a sentence (p. 366). Thus, when a sentence is presented both *with* and *without* a major constituent boundary, it is more difficult to comprehend the latter form. For example, Graff and Torrey (1966) present the importance of identifying constituent structure as follows:

Form A	Form B
During World War II even fantastic schemes received consideration if they gave promise of shortcoming the conflict.	During World War II even fantastic schemes received consideration if they gave promise of shortcoming the conflict.

In Form A, each line corresponds to a major constituent boundary unlike the lines in Form B. In the study by Graff and Torrey (1966), the participants presented with Form A (with its correct syntactic structures) showed better comprehension of the passages. This finding proves that the identification of constituent structure is vital to comprehension. When one reads passages, it is natural to pause at the boundaries between clauses. These passages or segments with correct syntactic structures are then recombined to generate a meaningful representation of the original sequence. The importance of 'parsing a sentence' or constituent structure is also confirmed by Jarvella (1971), Caplan (1972) and Aaronson and

Scarborough (1977). As for the characteristic of parsing, Anderson (2010, p. 362) describes that people process the meaning of a sentence one phrase at a time and maintain access to a phrase only while processing its meaning. He refers to this principle as 'immediacy of interpretation'. In other words, people, when processing a sentence, attempt to extract meaning out of each word as it arrives, and they do not wait until the end of a sentence or even the end of a phrase to decide how to interrupt a word.

The third and final stage is utilisation. In this stage, it is sometimes necessary for a listener to make different types of inferences to complete an interpretation of an utterance, especially since the actual meaning of an utterance is not always the same as what is stated. That is, to completely understand a sentence, a listener sometimes needs to make inferences and connections so that s/he can make the sentence more meaningful. In addition, mental representation is also required to comprehend the speaker's actual meaning. For example, in England, a sentence such as 'Were you born in a barn?' does not actually enquire whether the listener was born in a barn. Instead, it infers that if a person was born in a barn, then s/he is unaware of the custom of closing a door after entering/exiting a building. Thus, the actual and ironical meaning of the sentence is 'Shut the door!' Successful comprehension requires a finishing touch, called utilisation, after the perception and parsing stages. Figure 2.2 demonstrates the hierarchical model of Anderson's cognitive psychology theory (2010).

Figure 2.2 Hierarchical model of Anderson's cognitive psychology theory (2010)

2.1.3 Mental process in listening comprehension and cognitive psychology theory

Based on Anderson's theory[1], O'Malley et al. (1989) conducted a milestone study on listening strategy with 11 Hispanic intermediate students. They revealed that the mental processes of the students in listening comprehension actually parallel Anderson's (2010) cognitive psychology theory in four ways: 1) the students were listening for larger chunks, shifting their attention to individual words only when there was a breakdown in comprehension; 2) they utilised both top-down and bottom-up processing strategies, whereas ineffective listeners repeatedly attempted to determine the meanings of individual words; 3) they were adept at constructing meaningful sentences from the input received, even though the meaning slightly differed from that of the actual text and 4) they applied their knowledge in three areas, i.e. world knowledge, personal knowledge and self-questioning.

The theories of Schneider and Shiffrin (1977) and Anderson (2010) have commonalities in that both involve gradual steps in human information processing as well as language learning. In the next section, whether listening strategies improve learners' listening comprehension is argued.

2.1.4 Differences in the listening comprehension strategies by proficiency levels

In this section, clarifications in terms of listening strategies will be discussed according to several prominent studies. Although there were some early studies of listening strategies conducted in the 1970s, such as Brown (1977) and Flavell (1979), one of the earliest studies of EFL/ESL listening strategies is probably the study by DeFilippis (1980), who investigates listening strategies in French by focussing on 26 second-language listeners that are equally divided into two groups (i.e. 13 skilled and 13 less-skilled).

---

[1] The first edition was published in 1980.

Using the listening parts of a standardised test[2], he compares the listening strategies of both groups and observes major differences in the listening strategies of skilled and less-skilled listeners. For example, skilled listeners report an automatic flow of the auditory stimulus, and they apply keywords, inferences and grammar strategies, whereas less-skilled listeners use keywords and translation strategies as well as contextual inferences. He also reports that skilled listeners utilise five times more visualisation, three times more French–English cognates and two times more role identification compared to their less-skilled counterparts. His study was followed by numerous researchers in the 1980s such as Murphy (1985), Chamot (1987), Murphy (1987), O'Malley (1987), Rubin (1988), Rubin, Quinn and Enos (1988) and O'Malley, Chamot and Küpper (1989).

Adding to the findings of DeFilippis (1980), Goss (1982) reports that competent listeners are capable of using many strategies and knowing when to use them. Murphy (1985) also presents a different feature between more- and less-proficient listeners. The former tend to use a strategy called 'wide distribution' (an open and flexible use of strategies), whereas the latter frequently use a 'text heavy' strategy (which depends on the text and the consistent paraphrasing).

Furthermore, O'Malley et al. (1989) observe that effective listeners utilise both top-down and bottom-up processing strategies, whereas ineffective listeners become embedded in determining the meanings of individual words (p. 434). They also report that effective listeners notice when their attention falters and they make a deliberate effort to refocus on the listening task, whereas less-effective listeners encounter an unfamiliar word and make no effort to continue listening. Although Anderson's (2010) three-stage model is based on first language comprehension, his cognitive framework is extremely useful for understanding EFL/ESL listeners' difficulties since it can pinpoint where comprehension breaks down in

---

[2] The Modern Language Association Cooperative Foreign Language Test

cognitive processing. For example, less-effective listeners make no effort to continue listening because they have not fully acquired perceptual processing, which is the ability to decode acoustic information. Other significant differences between effective and ineffective listeners are also observed with regard to self-monitoring (or checking one's listening comprehension), elaboration (or correlating new information with prior knowledge or other ideas) and inference (or using information in a text to guess the meaning or complete the missing ideas) (O'Malley et al., 1989, p. 427).

The study by Ho (2006, p. 71) is consistent with the study by DeFilippis (1980) in which low-proficiency listeners significantly use the translation strategy more often than high-proficiency ones. Graham, Santos and Vanderplank (2008) also claim that strategy development seems to be related to proficiency levels. Their results show a high degree of stability of strategy use over six months, especially between the high and low scorers. They state that a certain pattern exists regarding strategy development. Inference and reliance on prior knowledge gradually declines (perhaps as learners' linguistic base increases), whereas the use of metacognitive strategies increases. However, the latter may be limited to more 'capable' learners and linked to the availability of processing capacity, which, in turn, may be related to linguistic knowledge.

Although both DeFilippis (1980) and O'Malley, Chamot and Küpper (1989) utilise different terms such as 'automatic flow' of the auditory stimulus, contextual inferencing strategy, grammar strategy, keyword strategy, translation strategy and top-down/bottom-up processing strategies, their research results point to one direction: metacognitive knowledge and its usage is the key to become a successful listener.

Flavell (1979, p. 906) defines metacognitive knowledge as 'that segment of stored world knowledge that has to do with people as cognitive creatures and with their diverse cognitive tasks, goals, actions, and experiences'. Metacognitive knowledge consists of three categories, i.e.

person knowledge, task knowledge and strategy knowledge. Vandergrift, Goh, Mareschal and Tafaghodtari (2006, pp. 433–434) describe them as follows:

i) Person knowledge: judgments about one's learning abilities and knowledge about internal and external factors, such as age, aptitude, gender and learning style, that affect the success or failure in one's learning.

ii) Task knowledge: knowledge about the purpose, demands and nature of learning tasks. It also includes knowledge of the procedures involved in accomplishing these tasks.

iii) Strategy knowledge: knowledge about strategies that may be effective in achieving learning goals.

There is a common consensus among researchers in learning that metacognition plays a key role. Numerous researchers, such as Palmer and Goetz (1988), Victori and Lockhart (1995), Winne (1995), Schoonen, Hulstijn and Bossers (1998), Boekaerts, Pintrich and Zeidner (2000), Zimmerman and Schunk (2001), Mokhtari and Reichard (2002), Bolitho et al. (2003) and Eilam and Aharon (2003), support that there is extensive evidence that learners' metacognition can directly affect the process and the outcome of their learning. Similarly, in the field of listening strategy, Goh (2002) introduces a concrete metacognitive knowledge about listening (Table 2.1).

Table 2.1   Metacognitive Knowledge about Listening (Vandergrift, Goh, Mareschal and Tafaghodtari, 2006)

Metacognitive knowledge		Examples from listening
Person knowledge	Knowledge about how factors such as age, aptitude, gender and learning style can influence language learning. It also includes beliefs about oneself as a learner	· Self-concepts and self-efficiency about listening · Specific listening problems, causes and possible solutions
Task knowledge	Knowledge about the purpose, the demands and the nature of learning tasks. It also includes knowledge of the procedures involved in accomplishing these tasks.	· Mental, affective and social process involved in listening · Skills (e.g. listening for details, gist) needed for completing listening tasks · Factors that influence listening (e.g. text, speaker) · Ways of improving listening outside class
Strategy knowledge	Knowledge about strategies that are likely to be effective in achieving learning goals	· General and specific strategies to facilitate comprehension and cope with difficulties · Strategies appropriate for specific types of listening · Ineffective strategies

Vandergrift, Goh, Mareschal and Tafaghodtari (2006, p. 435) claim that learners with high degrees of metacognitive awareness are better at processing, storing new information, finding the best ways to practice and reinforcing what they have learnt and that metacognitive abilities are a mental characteristic shared by successful learners. Goh (1997, 2002) and Vandergrift (2003) present numerous studies about learners' metacognitive knowledge in EFL/ESL listening with various procedures such as diaries, interviews and questionnaires. Results of these studies have shown that language learners possess knowledge about the listening process, albeit to varying degrees and that this knowledge appears to be linked to listening abilities (Vandergrift, Goh, Mareschal and Tafaghodtari, 2006, p. 436).

Chamot (1995, p. 18) describes that the failure of less-effective listeners to use appropriate strategies for the different phases of listening is due to limited metacognitive knowledge about selecting appropriate strategies for the task. Vandergrift (1997) also reports clear differences in the listening strategies of 21 French listeners (i.e. 10 successful and 11 unsuccessful) based on four variables, i.e. level of language proficiency, gender, listening ability and learning style. He also reports that the use of metacognitive strategies such as comprehension monitoring, problem identification and selective attention seem to be the key factors that distinguish the successful listeners from the less successful ones. However, the difference for gender was minimal, and the difference for learning style was inconclusive.

Goh (2000) also supports the importance of a cognitive framework in understanding learners' listening difficulties, because it specifies the point at which comprehension breaks down during cognitive processing. In turn, this knowledge makes it possible to trace the source of learners' listening difficulties and equips teachers with the skills to guide them towards overcoming such obstacles. She claims that understanding why some of the problems occur will naturally place teachers in a better position to guide learners in ways of coping with or overcoming some of their listening difficulties (p. 57).

Berne (2004) summarises the differences between more- and less-proficient listeners[3], as shown in Table 2.2.

---

[3] The descriptive and theoretical studies of Mendelsohn (1994, 1995), Vandergrift (1996, 1997 and 1999) and Field (1998) are excluded since none of these researchers empirically examined the effectiveness of their proposed approaches, as Berne (2004, p. 526) indicates.

Table 2.2   Differences between More- and Less-Proficient Listeners
(Berne, 2004, p. 525)

More-Proficient Listeners	Less-Proficient Listeners
use strategies more often	process input word by word
use a wide range of strategies	rely heavily on translation/key words as strategies
use strategies interactively	are negatively affected by linguistic and attentional constrains
are concerened with the overall rhetorical organisation of text	are concerned with definitions/pronunciation of words
are better able to: 　attend to larger chunks of input 　monitor/redirect attention 　grasp overall meaning of input 　guess meanings of words	make fewer inferences/elaborations
	do not verify their assumptions
	do not relate what they hear to previous experiences
use existing linguistics knowledge to aid comprehension	

Ho (2006, p. 69) observes that high-proficiency listeners employ 10 metacognitive strategies more frequently than the less proficient ones and that high-proficiency listeners are able to use the following strategies more frequently than their low-proficiency counterparts, i.e. self-management, self-monitoring, refocusing and self-evaluation. Again, the results are consistent with the findings of O'Malley, Chamot and Küpper (1989). In their study, they similarly assert that effective students are better at monitoring their attention than the less effective ones.

Vandergrift, Goh, Mareschal and Tafaghodtari (2006) conduct a survey regarding metacognitive awareness in listening by administering the MALQ[4]. They establish the following five factors based on the responses of 966 participants: 1) problem solving (guessing as well as monitoring the guesses), 2) planning and evaluation (preparing to listen and assessing success), 3) mental translation (translation from English to first language (L1) when listening), 4) person knowledge (confidence or anxiety and

---

[4] The questionnaire was designed by Vandergrift, Goh, Mareschal and Tafaghodtari (2006).

self-perception as a listener) and 5) directed attention (ways of concentrating on certain aspects of a task). These factors, which accounted for approximately 13% of the validity in the listeners' performance, suggest that approximately 90% of success in listening is based on additional factors. This also indicates the complexity of listening comprehension in English. Lynch (2009, pp. 82–83) claims that this finding is the most tangible outcome from two decades of research regarding metacognitive strategies in listening.

Baleghizadeh and Rahimi (2011) also confirm the relationship between metacognitive strategy use and listening test performance through their study of 82 Iranian EFL university students based on three instruments, i.e. the MALQ, the Academic Motivation Scale and the listening parts of the Test of English as a Foreign Language® (TOEFL®). In addition, they found a statistically significant and positive correlation between metacognitive strategy use and listening performance. Metacognitive knowledge is firmly linked to listening ability (p. 66).

In the study of Graham, Santos and Vanderplank (2011), they investigate the development of the listening proficiency and strategic behaviour of 15 lower-intermediate learners of French in England for six months with two methods, i.e. recall protocols and strategy elicitation. First, the participants listened to two different audio recordings on the same topic and were asked to write in English everything they had understood. Then, they listened to four different texts and had to answer multiple-choice questions in English for strategy elicitation to capture participants' usual way of listening. They were requested to verbalise how they were about comprehending the text and answering the questions as fully as possible. The six- month study confirms that the use of metacognitive strategies increases with higher listening proficiency and that both inferencing and reliance on prior knowledge appear to become less prominent as learners' listening proficiency increases. These results match the studies of Graham et al. (2008), Vogley (1995) and Vandergrift (1997, 1998).

Hamamoto et al.'s (2013) study on listening strategy with 441 participants (169 high-level listeners, 152 intermediate listeners and 120 low-level listeners) shows that there is a clear difference in listening strategy use based on listening ability and proficiency level. The high-level listeners prefer the use of metacognitive strategies involving selective attention, advance organisation and self-management as well as cognitive strategies such as top-down inferencing, whereas the low-level listeners use only a limited number of listening strategies such as bottom-up cognitive strategies and inferencing. The intermediate listeners show tendencies similar to the high-level listeners in the use of advanced organisation and self-management of metacognitive strategies, whereas they were similar to the low-level listeners in inferencing.

With many other studies such as Henrichsen (1984), Murphy (1985), O'Malley (1987), Rubin, Quinn and Enos (1988), O'Malley, Chamot and Küpper (1989), Vann and Abraham (1990), Nagano (1991), Rost and Ross (1991), Oxford (1993), Rubin (1994), Buck (1995), Chamot (1995), Vogely (1995), Moreira (1996), Chao (1997), Park (1997), Chien and Wei (1998), Goh (1998), Peters (1999), Ozeki (2000), Goh (2002), Shirono (2003), Wang (2002), Vandergrift (2003), Chang and Read (2006), Ho (2006), Graham, Santos and Vanderplank (2008, 2011), Chang (2009), Cross (2010), Baleghizadeh and Rahimi (2011) and Ueda (2013), it can be concluded that the differences in EFL/ESL listening strategies depend on listening abilities and proficiency and that both metacognitive knowledge and its usage are the key to become a successful listener.

However, this raises the following question: If listening strategies and metacognitive strategies used by more-proficient listeners are taught to less-proficient listeners, then would they improve their listening comprehension? This issue will be discussed in the following section.

2.2 Previous Research Arguments
2.2.1 Teachability and effectiveness of explicit strategies instruction

As described earlier, it has become clear that there are differences in listening strategy use based on listening ability and proficiency level. For example, high-level listeners seem to use more metacognitive strategies more often, while low-level listeners are apparently able to use only a limited number of listening strategies. In regard to the aforementioned question (If listening strategies and metacognitive strategies used by more-proficient listeners are taught to less-proficient listeners, then would they improve their listening comprehension?), some studies have responded with a 'yes' (Rubin, 1994; Cross, 2009; Graham, Santos and Vanderplank, 2011), whereas others are 'sceptical' (Field, 2008; Lynch, 2009).

Rost and Ross (1991) claim that teaching listening strategies is effective. They conducted research on listening strategies with 72 Japanese listeners (i.e. 40 high-proficiency listeners and 32 low-proficiency listeners). The results indicate that strategies used by the high-proficiency listeners could be successfully taught to low-proficiency listeners (p. 236).

Rost and Wilson (2013, p. 244) also state that it is advantageous to teach listening strategies either directly (i.e. naming and demonstrating the strategy) or indirectly (i.e. coaching students on the ways to improve their listening without naming them). Many other researchers such as Rubin and Thompson (1992, 1993), Thompson and Rubin (1996), Mendelsohn (1994, 1995) and Buck (1995) support that explicit strategies are teachable and effective.

However, the teachability and the effectiveness of explicit strategies instruction were first questioned by Tudor (1996). He argues that 'it would be misleading to assume that these strategies can be neatly pedagogised and "taught" to learners in a straightforward manner' (p. 39). Field (1998) also claims that it has not been conclusively demonstrated that this type of strategy training is effective and that attempts to teach strategies individually based on the analysis–synthesis principle have not necessarily led to greater overall listening competence. Field (1998, p. 115) questions the findings of Rubin (1994) and Chamot (1995) in which only two out of their 12 studies showed that improvement had occurred. Two years later, Field (2000, p. 32) raised the following question: Can we actually teach the strategies that a learner needs in order to handle gaps in understanding? He claims that the research evidence on listening is less than conclusive and if strategies, such as monitoring one's own understanding, identifying keywords and predicting text context, are taught separately, then learners may show improvement in their handling of the individual strategy but not necessarily improve overall as listeners. Interestingly, he indicates that no matter how good learners become at using a certain strategy, they will have difficulty combining it with other strategies and using it *appropriately*[5] to meet the demands of a particular listening task.

Ozeki (2000) examines the effectiveness of learning strategies that Japanese female college students frequently used for listening tasks and observes the following:

i) Students do not often utilise listening strategies themselves.
ii) Students rarely use metacognitive strategies such as planning, directed attention, selective attention or self-evaluation.
iii) Students are frequently distracted by unknown words and they lose focus.
iv) Students are not used to selective attention, pre-reading true and false questions and choosing the keywords in questions before actually listening to the material.
v) Students seldom use the self-evaluating strategy unless the teacher includes it as a classroom activity (pp. 95–96).

As Oxford (1990) signifies, Ozeki (2000) claims that students who believe that the teacher is the authoritative source of knowledge lack the

---

[5] The emphasis was made by Field (2000, p. 32).

initiative to learn on their own, and that they rarely use metacognitive strategies, which can enable them to plan, monitor and evaluate their learning.

Berne (2004, p. 526) suggests the following: Listening instruction must be differentiated by level. Field (1998) also argues that strategy training may not benefit learners who are initially weak strategy users. Thus, it may not be appropriate to teach the same types of strategies to less- and more-proficient listeners since they have different needs and knowledge bases.

Although Graham, Santos and Vanderplank (2008) claim that strategy development is related to proficiency issues, their results also show a high degree of stability in strategy use. Analyses of their commentaries show that students remained fairly consistent in their strategy use over a six-month period, thus leading the researchers to conclude that listening strategy use is relatively stable and closely tied to proficiency level (p. 66).

Other researchers, such as Rees-Miller (1993), Mendelsohn (1994), Tudor (1996), Field (2008) and Lynch (2009) claim that there is insufficient evidence about the effects of instructing listening strategies, whereas Thompson and Rubin (1996), Park (1997) and Vandergrift (1999), Carrier (2003), Graham and Macaro (2008), Cross (2009) and Suzuki (2009) still support that explicit strategies are teachable and effective.

The next section discusses one way to approach and tackle this question of whether listening strategies improve learners' EFL/ESL listening comprehension.

2.2.2 Lack of a standardised test to measure participants' proficiency and compare results

This section explores the importance of standardised language proficiency tests, which are still the subject of wide-ranging debate among researchers. In this study, standardised tests are defined as any language proficiency tests that are reliable, international, popular, relatively easy to access and capable of being compared/converted other tests. Such tests are crucial for two reasons, i.e. to define participants' proficiency levels *before* an study and evaluate the effect of an study objectively and scientifically. The majority of previous studies on listening strategy have compared more- and less-successful listeners. This is because, as Wu (1998) indicates, the preferred method in the field of testing assessment is to compare the top and bottom groups, ranging from 25 to 33% of the samples. In addition, the gap between the two groups is prominent, and the differences are easy to compare. Therefore, it is quite natural to compare these two groups.

However, these studies contained significant variations and ambiguities and employed only a limited number of standardised tests for classification purposes. Few standardised tests were used to determine the proficiency level of the participants *before* studies were conducted. In addition, researchers' classifications of learners as more- or less-proficient listeners vary significantly across studies and, as mentioned above, the lack of a standardised measure of listening proficiency can diminish the overall generalisability of the findings since it cannot ensure that each study measures the same parameters. The studies that do not utilise a standardised test to measure participants' proficiency and compare the results can be divided into four types: 1) a study without any tests, 2) a study with a test which does not measure listening comprehension but other skills such as reading and mathematical skills, 3) a study with a local/minor test and 4) a study with a standardised test but no description/definition regarding the participants' classification.

For example, no standardised test was used in the following studies: Fujiwara (1990), Bacon (1992a, 1992b), Laviosa (1992), Goh (1997, 2000), Vandergrift (2003), Zhang and Goh (2006), Graham, Santos and Vanderplank (2008, 2011), Graham and Macaro (2008), Cross (2009, 2010) and Vandergrift and Tafaghodtari (2010). Rubin, Quinn and Enos (1988) employ the California Assessment Program in their study. However, it is a test of reading, writing and basic mathematical skills, but not a test to assess listening comprehension. Thomson and Rubin (1996) use the speaking ability section from the American Council on The Teaching of Foreign Languages (ACTFL). Vogely (1995), Ozeki (2000), Shirono (2003), Carrier (2003) and Suzuki (2009) use some tests, but they are not standardised tests. Thus, it is almost impossible to scientifically and objectively compare the participants' comprehension levels and research results. Chang (2008) uses the TOEIC® to define the participants' proficiency levels but did not mention the basis of the definitions.

Without the use of a standardised test, those categorised as more-successful listeners in one study might be considered as intermediate in another, whilst those categorised as intermediate in one study might be classified as less successful in another (Table 2.3).

Table 2.3   Comparison of Some Standardised Test Scores/Grades[6]

TOEFL®	TOEFL®iBT	IELTS	Cambridge	TOEIC®	EIKEN
677	120	9.0	CPE	990	
650	115	7.5–8.5		890	
600	100	6.0–7.0	CAE	660–810	Grade 1
550	80				
500	61	5.5	FCE	590	Grade Pre-1
470	52	5.0		450–520	
		4.5			
450	45	3.5–4.0	PET	310–380	Grade Pre-2 to Grade 2
		2.5–3.0	KET		Grade 3
		1.0–2.0	Young Learners	220	Grade 4 to 5

---

[6] The TOEFL® iBT test measures the ability to use and understand English at the university level, i.e. listening, reading, speaking and writing skills for academic tasks. The International English Language Testing System (IELTS) is designed to assess the language ability of candidates who want to study or work where English is the primary language of communication. The IELTS is accepted by thousands of organisations in more than 135 countries. Cambridge = Cambridge English Language Assessment, CPE = Certificate in Proficiency in English, CAE = Certificate in Advanced English, FCE = First Certificate in English, PET = Preliminary English Test, KET = Key English Test and EIKEN = a test in practical English proficiency, which is Japan's most widely recognised English language assessment.

For example, although O'Malley et al.'s study (1989) is one of the first experimental studies on language learning strategies instruction that compared more- and less-effective listeners, the number of participants therein is only 11, and no standardised test is used to define their competence in English *prior* to the study. In addition, the participants' proficiency levels are defined by a mere school district placement test. There are additional studies in which tests have not been used to assess the proficiency level of the participants *before* the study and even if a test has been used, in most cases, it is very minor or local to provide objective information about participants' comprehension levels.

To encourage the use of standardised tests, they must be easily accessible outside the designated district and be either low cost or free. Moreover, the scores of standardised tests must be convertible to those of international tests such as the TOEFL® or TOEIC®. If participants' comprehension levels *before* a study are not determined objectively through standardised tests, then the results of the study cannot be considered as objective. Furthermore, even when employing a standardised test, Rubin (1994) proposes that the division of groups or participants should be clearly described. 'Although DeFilippis (1980) used a standard instrument, the rationale for selecting the point where she divided the group is not clear' (p. 212). O'Malley and Chamot (1990, p.11) define successful listeners as 'those who report the greatest frequency, variety and sophistication of language learning strategies'. However, the range of successful learners varies depending on the instructor, and participants can be categorised differently across studies. Therefore, it is essential that every study should utilise an independent measure of success.

The second important reason for employing standardised tests is that it would be difficult to compare the results with those of other studies without such tests and regardless of how many studies are conducted, EFL/ESL listening would not progress meaningfully. Rubin (1994) expresses that 'most of the research results are based on listening comprehension measures that have not been standardised, making it difficult to compare results' (p. 199) and 'most studies use either teacher judgment, course level or performance on a non-standard test' (p. 206). In addition, she states that studies that do not utilise standardised tests cannot provide firm conclusions, and comparisons can be problematic for determining proficiency. Rubin's point is supported by Mendelsohn (1995) who stated that '...there is a need for *diagnostic tests*[7] to assess learners' proficiency levels' (p. 137). Furthermore, Berne (1993, 2004) addresses the importance of defining the categorisation of participants:

> The lack of a common, standardized measure of
> listening proficiency across these studies is
> problematic in that it may diminish the generalizability
> of the findings.... Thus, we cannot be sure that each
> of these studies is measuring the same thing when
> assessing listening proficiency. In addition,
> listening comprehension performance may vary
> according to the task used to assess it. (Berne, 1993)

> Therefore, in order to enhance the generalizability
> of their findings, researchers may want to consider
> adopting a common set of well-tested, objective
> criteria for assessing listening proficiency... (Berne, 2004, p. 523)

As introduced above, a standardised test is essential for enhancing the credibility of a study's findings. In this study, the listening parts of the TOEIC® are adopted as an objective measure for assessing the participants' listening proficiency before/after the studies as well as the experimental results.

---

[7] The emphasis was made by Mendelsohn (1995).

2.2.3 Lack of studies about the intermediate level

Although there has been progress in the field of EFL/ESL listening strategy since 1980, many issues still remain unresolved. One of the reasons is that the majority of the studies have focussed on the differences between more- and less-successful listeners (DeFilippis, 1980; Murphy, 1987; O'Malley, Chamot and Küpper, 1989; Rost and Ross, 1991; Moreira, 1996; Vandergrift, 1997; Goh, 2000; Shirono, 2003; Graham, Santos and Vanderplank, 2008; Vandergrift and Tafaghodtari, 2010). However, when examining the majority of EFL/ESL learners in listening, especially in Asia and South America, they fall into the intermediate level, as described in Chapter 1. There are some EFL/ESL listening strategy studies that have focussed on intermediate learners, but the findings have been inconclusive. For example, Murphy (1985) studies the ESL listening strategies of more- and less-proficient intermediate learners based on their oral and written responses to listening selections. He concludes that listening is an interpretive language process in which various strategies are interwoven and that both textual and non-textual information (combined with the strategies used) determines the listener's interpretation of what s/he hears. To select the participants, he used the Michigan Test of Aural Comprehension, the Listening Proficiency Rating Scale for Adult Migrant Education and the City University of New York Reading Assessment Test (CRAT). However, it is not described how they were classified as intermediate learners. Furthermore, the CRAT is primarily a reading assessment test.

O'Malley (1987) investigates the effects of learning strategies training on ESL learning with 75 intermediate high school students, but they are chosen based on the results of school district placement procedures. Again, it is not described how they are categorised as intermediate learners, and the placement test is not a standardised test. Thus, it may never be clear whether this study actually focussed on intermediate learners.

Vandergrift (1997) focuses on the differences in strategy use amongst novice and intermediate learners of French using data elicited through think-aloud protocols. He claims that intermediate listeners use a higher percentage of metacognitive strategies than novice listeners. However, only six intermediate listeners are categorised as 'more-successful listeners', whilst only one listener is categorised as 'less successful'. In addition, it is not explained how they are classified as intermediate learners. Furthermore, the ACTFL oral proficiency interview (OPI) is used to select the participants. Nonetheless, the OPI is not a test to assess a learner's listening proficiency but one's *oral* proficiency. This raises the question of why the official ACTFL Listening Test for Professionals was not employed since it is a global assessment listening test that can be used for all levels.

Ho (2006) examines the EFL listening strategies of 190 high-intermediate Taiwanese students by using the five levels of the General English Proficiency Test (GEPT), i.e. elementary, intermediate, high-intermediate, advanced and superior. The GEPT is a test of English language proficiency that was commissioned by Taiwan's Ministry of Education in 1999. Although the details are described as to how they are categorised as intermediate learners (e.g. those who ranked in the top 30% are placed in the high-listening proficiency group, whereas the bottom 30% are placed in the low-listening proficiency group), it does not explain whether the test scores are able to be converted into the scores of the TOEIC®, the TOEFL® or other standardised tests.

Chen (2007) investigates the EFL listening strategies of 64 Taiwanese students who were selected according to their scores on the Secondary Level English Proficiency® (SLEP®) test. In this case, 56 participants are ranked as low-intermediate on the listening comprehension section (30th–50th percentile), four as high-intermediate (50th–70th percentile) and four as advanced (70th percentile and higher). The SLEP® test was developed by the Educational Testing Service, and it *was* a standardised multiple-choice test designed to measure both listening and reading comprehension skills of non-native English speakers *until* 2012. As of 30th June 2012, the SLEP® test has been discontinued, and no materials can be obtained. Again, this study does not explain whether the test scores can be converted into those of other standardised tests.

Graham, Santos and Vanderplank (2008, 2011) investigate listening comprehension and strategy use of British lower-intermediate learners of French. They are categorised as lower-intermediate since they are preparing for a lower-intermediate examination—the Advanced Subsidiary examination, which focuses on traditional study skills. Their listening proficiency is assessed using two different audio recordings of comparable difficulty on the topic of holidays. Again, it does not explain whether these test scores can be converted into those of other standardised tests.

Chang (2008) studies the strategies of EFL students and how they adjusted these strategies in response to various listening tasks. She recruited 22 Taiwanese students (beginner and low-intermediate) based on their TOEIC® scores. However, it does not describe how they are classified as intermediate. Similarly, Chang (2009) examines 75 Chinese EFL learners' test-taking strategies and their relationship with listening performance using a 40-item listening test. The participants are classified according to their scores on the listening test. The highest possible score on the listening test is 40, and those who score between 21 and 29 are categorised as intermediate. However, since the test is not a standardised listening test, there is no way to compare these findings with other research results objectively.

Finally, Chang and Read (2006) investigate the effects of four types of listening support, i.e. previewing the test questions, repetition of the input, providing background knowledge about the topic and vocabulary instruction. They clarify the participants' levels by using the mean scores of the listening parts of the TOEIC®. For example, those who receive scores between 38.67 and 40.40 (out of 100) are categorised as intermediate. This score range, equivalent to 235 to 245 (out of 495) in the listening parts of the TOEIC®, is consistent with the definition of intermediate listeners in the present study. Their findings show that the most effective type of support was providing information about the topic. This is followed sequentially by repetition of the input, the fact that the learners' level of listening proficiency has a significant interaction effect (particularly in the case of question preview) and that vocabulary instruction is the least useful form of support, regardless of proficiency level.

Based on the aforementioned evidence, limited studies have objectively focussed on intermediate learners. Berne (2004, p. 526) indicates that listening instruction must be differentiated by level and that it may be inappropriate to teach the same strategies to more- and less-proficient listeners since they have different needs and knowledge bases. Therefore, additional studies regarding the types of more effective teaching methods for intermediate learners are required and essential in the field of ESL/EFL listening strategies. Hence, the purpose of the present study is to discover these types of teaching methods for intermediate learners and how to implement them pedagogically. As Mendelsohn (1995) suggests, the task of language teachers is to teach students 'how to listen' by using strategies that will lead to better comprehension rather than merely giving them an opportunity to listen (p. 133).

Chapter 3: Study I—Dictation Training and Listening Strategy Training

3.1 Hypotheses

This study concerns the effective teaching methods for intermediate listeners. To investigate this issue, the effectiveness of two different teaching methods are first examined in Study I.

As stated in the previous chapter, there are two types of human information processing, i.e. controlled and automatic human information processing. The former involves a sequence of cognitive activities under active control, whereas the latter involves a sequence of cognitive activities that occurs automatically without the necessity of active control (Schneider and Shiffrin, 1977; Shiffrin and Schneider, 1977).

Similarly, in a cognitive framework of language comprehension, there are multiple levels, as Anderson (2010) proposes: perception, parsing and utilisation, with perception being the lowest. *Perception* or speech recognition is the encoding of the acoustic message, and it involves segmenting phonemes from the continuous speech stream (p. 52). During this phase in listening, one focuses closely on input, and the sounds are retained in echoic memory (Goh, 2000, p. 57). In *parsing*, words are transformed into a mental representation of the combined meaning of the words. This occurs when an utterance is segmented according to syntactic structures or meaning cues. These segments are then recombined to generate a meaningful representation of the original sequence. This mental representation, related to existing knowledge, is stored in a long-term memory as proportions or schemata during the third phase, i.e. *utilisation*. At this level, listeners may draw different types of inferences to complete the interpretation and make it more personally meaningful (p. 57).

During the initial stage of foreign language learning, learners must consciously focus on new elements, such as different phonemes and words from their first language, until these elements become more familiar to them. These two theories claim that there are gradual steps in both human information processing and language learning.

Although many researchers report that teaching various types of listening strategies are useful, these listening strategies might be very complicated for intermediate listeners since they may still be at the level of controlled processing and perception. Therefore, Study I addresses the following question: Out of the two types of listening training (i.e. dictation training and listening strategy training), which one would be more effective for intermediate listeners? Based on the two aforementioned theories and this research question, the following two hypotheses are formulated.

H-1 For intermediate listeners, dictation training is more effective than listening strategy training.

As stated earlier, Schneider and Shiffrin (1977) propose two types of cognitive processing, i.e. controlled and automatic human information processing. Dictation and identification of individual words are considered to be controlled processing (bottom-up processing) since they are firmly related to phonemic decoding. In this study, dictation refers to the act of listening to one sentence or a very short passage in English and writing it down. Since the participants listen only to one sentence or a very short passage, the relevance of their grammatical knowledge or background context is minimal. Listeners utilise mainly acoustic information to interpret spoken words and phrases.

Conversely, employing listening strategies is regarded as automatic processing (top-down processing), because it is difficult to achieve the required capacity for employing listening strategies unless the identification of individual words becomes automatic. Therefore, intermediate listeners in Study I may find dictation training more adequate since there are gradual steps in both human information processing and language learning.

According to Anderson's (2010) cognitive psychology theory, parsing is the second stage after perception in which 'words are transformed into a mental representation of the combined meaning of the words'. In addition, parsing only occurs when a listener segments an utterance according to syntactic structures or meaning cues. Thus, Study I postulates that dictation training is more effective than listening strategy training for intermediate listeners.

H-2 For low-intermediate listeners, dictation training is more effective.

In Study I, intermediate listeners are divided into the following two groups:

i) Low-intermediate listeners: those who scored between 166 and 249 on the listening parts of the TOEIC® in Week 1.

ii) Upper-intermediate listeners: those who scored between 250 and 330 on the listening parts of the TOEIC® in Week 1.

For low-intermediate listeners, dictation training might be much more effective since they have not reached the level where perception and parsing occur automatically. In addition, they need active control and conscious attention for perception, whereas upper-intermediate listeners might be in the early stages of becoming skilled listeners. Thus, they may not find basic training on perception, such as dictation, beneficial.

3.2 Method
3.2.1 Participants

The participants in Study I consisted of 108 first-year students (in the Faculty of Economics) at a Japanese private university who were administered the listening parts of the TOEIC® in April 2012. Only those who scored between 166 and 330 were selected as the participants in Study I.

Study I - Dictation Training and Listening Strategy Training

In this study, the TOEIC® was employed to classify the participants' proficiency levels, but their levels could be converted into other standardised tests such as the EIKEN, IELTS and TOEFL®[8] (Table 3.1).

Table 3.1 Conversion Table of the TOEIC® Scores into Those of Other Standardised Tests

EIKEN	IELTS	TOEIC®	TOEFL® iBT	TOEFL® CBT	TOEFL® PBT
			120	300	677
Grade 1	7.0–7.5	990	111	273	641
		810	91	233	578
Grade Pre-1	5.0–6.0	740	82	217	554
Grade 2	4.0–4.5	520	53	153	477
Grade Pre-2	3.5–4.0	400	40	121	435
Grade 3	3.0	365	38	113	423
Grade 4	2.0–2.5	260	28	87	386
Grade 5	1.5–2.0				

None of the participants' major subject was English, and the classes were part of the regular English curriculum. The participants were divided into three groups, i.e. 10 in the control group (CG), which was part of the general English class; 52 in the dictation training group (DTG), with half of them belonging to the EFL listening class and the other half belonging to the EFL reading class and 46 in the listening strategy training group (LSTG), which was part of the EFL reading class. All the lessons were presented in English as per the policy of the faculty. Initially, there were more participants, but only those who attended all 15 classes between April and July 2012 were selected for Study I. Table 3.2 summarises the means, standard deviations (SDs) and relative values of these three groups in Week 1.

---

[8] PBT = paper-based test
CBT = computer-based test
TOEIC® score × 0.348 + 296 = TOEFL® PBT score

Table 3.2 Numbers, Means and SDs of the CG, DTG and LSTG in Week 1 of Study I

Groups	N	Mean	SD
CG	10	214.50	41.66
DTG	52	230.19	28.90
LSTG	46	241.30	32.41

A one-way analysis of variance (ANOVA) was conducted for their scores of the listening parts of the TOEIC®, and the results show that there was significance amongst these three groups ($F(2, 105) = 3.474, p < 0.05$). However, using Ryan's method for multiple comparisons, no significance amongst these three groups was observed.

Table 3.3 Results of Ryan's Method on the Three Groups before Study I

	CG	DTG	LSTG
mean :	214.50	230.19	241.30
n :	10	52	46

pair	r	nominal level	t	p	sig.
LSTG - CG	3	0.02	2.42	0.02	n.s.
LSTG - DTG	2	0.03	1.73	0.09	n.s.
DTG - CG	2	0.03	1.43	0.15	n.s.

$MSe = 1004.69, df = 105$, significance level $= 0.05$

3.2.2 Materials

For the DTG, materials were designed based on a textbook by Rost and Stratton (2001). They consisted of various patterns of reductions and contractions (for more details, see Appendix B). For the LSTG, materials were designed by the present author to aid in the acquisition of the various

Study I - Dictation Training and Listening Strategy Training

types of listening strategies (for more details, see Appendix C).

3.2.3 Procedure

In Week 1 of the first term in 2012, 108 participants were selected based on their TOEIC® listening scores. From Weeks 2 to 14, both the DTG and LSTG participants were trained for 30 minutes[9] (with instructions in Japanese) as part of the 90-minute regular class. The procedure of the dictation training included the following three steps.

In Step 1, the DTG participants were first informed about the purpose and subject of the training, after which they listened to the relevant parts of the CD (attached to the textbook) only once. Whilst listening, they dictated some words/phrases/short sentences on the provided handouts, which the present author had created based on the text book.

In Step 2, the participants viewed the answers whilst listening to the CD for a second time to combine the words/phrases/short sentences that they were unable to dictate *with* the acoustic information.

In Step 3, the participants listened to the CD a third time *without* looking at the answers to comprehend the words/phrases or short sentences that they were unable to dictate purely through the acoustic information.

The LSTG participants were first instructed on the logical aspects of the relevant listening strategies for that lesson. Then, they performed listening tasks that involved applying the instructed listening strategies, after which they were provided with the answers and pertinent feedback.

In Week 2, the concepts of content and function words were introduced: what they are and what types of words they comprise (see Week 2 on p. 189 in Appendix C for details). The data for my study about the MALQ (see 4.4.4 on p.88 in Chapter 4 and 5.4.5 on p.128 in Chapter 5 for details) show that many Japanese learners of English tend to stop listening when faced with a difficulty in understanding spoken English. By explaining

---

[9] Due to the inflexible class syllabus, only 30 minutes were allowed for the study.

that catching only content words is sufficient for understanding meaning, students learnt that it is not necessary to listen to every single word and that it is vital to keep listening even if they miss some words. Next, Exercise 1 introduced five new words (see Week 2 on p. 189 in Appendix C for details). The participants were instructed that the definitions for these words were in the CD, and they were to listen to the CD and fill in the blanks. The CD was played three times, following which the answers were shown with an overhead camera (OHC). The participants were then shown the definition of each word with only the definition's content words (i.e. function words were hidden) and asked whether they could understand them. They were also asked whether they could understand the definitions with only their function words (i.e. content words were hidden). Through this exercise, the participants realised that they did not have to listen to every single word for effective comprehension.

In Week 3, both working memory and note taking were introduced (see Week 3 on p.190 in Appendix C for details). First, three mobile numbers were read out by the author, and the participants were asked whether they could remember any of them. Through this exercise, the participants learnt how limited the capacity of working memory is, and how quickly we forget what we hear. They also learnt that note taking and listening skills are firmly interrelated, since it is impossible to *look* back in listening as one can in reading. Next, the participants were taught how to take notes whilst listening using marks, abbreviations, numbers, etc.

In Week 4, participants were introduced to inference. They learnt that all necessary information is not always stated, so listeners must sometimes infer the speaker's intended meaning from the given information. In listening such given information could include the pitch and tone of the speaker's voice, grammar, vocabulary and background knowledge. Next, five questions were presented, and the script was read out by the author five times (see Week 4 on p.191 in Appendix C for details). The answers were then shown with an OHC and explained. For example, based on the following sentences and words, it is possible to infer that Marisa is in a bathroom.

> Marisa was lying down looking at a reading book.
> The room was full of steam.
> soap
> a splash

For those who do not know the shape of a western-style bathtub, a picture was shown so that the participants could understand that one could actually lie down in a bathtub.

In Week 5, inference was further explored along with redundancy. The participants were instructed that it is possible to infer what was said through the active use of grammatical knowledge, vocabulary, background knowledge, etc. Then, Sentences 1, 2 and 3 in Exercise 1 were given to the participants on a handout (see Week 5 on p.192 in Appendix C for details). Without listening to the CD, they were asked to choose or write the correct answers. Next, the answers were shown with an OHC and explained. Finally, the CD was played once.

Redundancy was also introduced in Week 5. As previously noted, it is impossible to *look* back in listening like reading. The participants were taught that any speaker who knows the limitations of listening will relate important information slowly, repeatedly and loudly, and sometimes rephrase it to ensure that the information is understandable to the listener. After a short explanation of these ideas, the CD was played three times for Exercise 2, in which the participants were to fill in the blanks on an exercise sheet again. Then, the answers were shown with an OHC and explained.

In Week 6, discourse markers were introduced. First, the concept of discourse markers was explained along with how to use them to predict how the topic of the discourse will proceed. Next, the CD was played, and for Exercise 1, the participants were asked to write down three discourse markers that they had heard. Then, the answers were shown with an OHC and explained.

Following this, the participants listened to a short lecture about addictive substances and were asked to name three addictive substances and five examples of the first addictive substance (see Exercise 2 of Week 6 on pp. 193-194 in Appendix C for details). The CD was played once. Then, the answers were shown with an OHC and explained using the highlighted words and phrases (see the details in script of Exercise 2 of Week 6 in Appendix C).

In Week 7, the importance of background knowledge was presented. The author read out the script for Exercise 1 once, and the participants were asked to answer the question. Since almost no student could answer it, a picture of an ice cream van was shown, and the function of an ice cream van was explained (see Week 7 on p.195 in Appendix C for details). The manner in which they arrive in residential areas, playing cheerful music to attract children's attention, was also explained. Finally, the script was read out again, and the answer was explained.

The importance of adjustment was also introduced in Week 7 (see Week 7 on p.195 in Appendix C for details). The data for my study about the MALQ (see 4.4.4 on p.88 in Chapter 4 and 5.4.5 on p.128 in Chapter 5 for details) prove that not all learners of English can quickly adjust their interpretations whilst listening, even if they realise they had not understood something correctly. However, it is vital to adjust one's interpretation quickly in such situations. After this short instruction, the author read out the script ① of Exercise 2 (see Exercise 2 of Week 7 on p.195 in Appendix C for details). Then, the participants were asked to choose an answer from the multiple choices in ①. Next, the author read out the script ②. The participants were then asked to choose an answer from the multiple choices in ②. They were freely allowed to change their answer from their previous choice. The same procedure was repeated till ⑤. The answer was then shown with an OHC and explained.

Study I - Dictation Training and Listening Strategy Training

In Week 8, inference was presented again. First, the participants were divided roughly into two groups, i.e. Group A and B. Group A was given a handout entitled 'A prisoner plans his escape', and Group B was given another handout entitled 'A wrestler in a tight corner'. The participants were instructed not to show their handouts to anybody. Next, a list of words, which were boxed (see details in the script for Week 8 on p.196 in Appendix C), was given to ease the vocabulary problem. The participants could check their definitions with their dictionaries if anything was unclear. The script of a short story was then read out three times by the author, and the participants were asked to write a summary of the short story in Japanese. Some of the participants in both groups were asked to present their summaries. Despite having listened to the same story the same number of times, their summaries were quite different between Group A and B. Finally, it was revealed that they were actually given the same story with two different titles, and the participants realised how a title can influence one's comprehension and even the definitions of the same words.

In Week 9, the importance of knowledge in vocabulary, visual aids/information and background knowledge was introduced. No handouts were given at this stage. First, the script was read out once by the author, and the participants were asked to roughly state its subject matter. Most of them could not do so. Next, they were given highlighted words, and they checked their definitions with their dictionaries, and the script was read out by the present author once more (see the script of Week 9 on p.197 in Appendix C for details). Again, the participants were asked to state its subject matter. Then, a handout with a sketch (shown in Week 9 on p. 197 in Appendix C) was provided. The script was read out once more by the author, and the participants were asked to state its subject matter. Finally, a concept from the script, a mechanism of septal defect, was roughly explained. The script was then read out once again by the author, and the participants were asked to state its subject matter. Through these gradual steps, the participants experienced the importance of knowledge in vocabulary, visual aids/information and background knowledge, since they came to understand the context better each time they were provided with additional definitions, visual aids and background knowledge.

Week 10 focussed on scanning. Scanning is amongst the vital listening strategies for obtaining specific information. The participants were instructed on the importance of screening for what should be focussed on *prior to* listening. As a concrete procedure, they learnt to read the questions and multiple choice items before listening and to highlight or underline the content words (see the details in Week 10 on pp.198-199 in Appendix C). After this instruction, words were highlighted and shown with an OHC. Next, the participants listened to the CD once and answered the questions. Then, they were shown with an OHC and explained.

In Week 11, the participants received training in skimming. Like scanning, skimming is amongst the vital listening strategies for obtaining a rough idea of the topic. A handout was distributed to the participants without any explanation, and they were questioned about what they were going to do. Since most of the participants had taken the TOEIC® before this training, they could easily guess with a glance. The concept of skimming was then introduced. The CD was played once, and the answer was shown with an OHC and explained (see Week 11 on p.200 in Appendix C for details).

In Week 12, listening literacy was explained. Many learners of English in Japan typically trust the content of what they listen to in English. This is because English is a foreign language in Japan, so the content of much of what learners listen to in the English classroom has been revised and screened by both the lecturers and the textbook companies. Thus, learners usually do not have to doubt whether the content they are listening to is accurate. However, this is not always the case in reality. First, a handout was given to each participant without an explanation of what they were going to learn that day. The CD was played once, and the participants were asked to choose the answer. Most of them chose an answer, even though there was no correct answer amongst the multiple choices (see Week 12 on

Study I - Dictation Training and Listening Strategy Training

p.201 in Appendix C for details). They were then asked to reveal their answers. The participants then learnt that there was actually no answer; thus, it is important to confirm what they listen to.

In Week 13, scanning instruction continued. A review of scanning from Week 10 was conducted, and the CD was played once. Then, the answers were shown with an OHC and explained (see Week 13 on p.202 in Appendix C for details).

In Week 14, scanning was further introduced. A review of scanning in Weeks 10 and 13 was conducted first, and the participants were asked to highlight the content words before listening. The CD was played once, and the answers were shown with an OHC and explained. For example, the three multiple choices in yellow are categorised as places, those in green as topics and the boxed ones as speakers/persons (see Exercise 1 of Week 14 on p.203 in Appendix C for details). Then, the participants realised that recognising these categories before listening made choosing the correct answer much easier. Thus, they learnt the vital importance of scanning the given information as much as possible before listening.

In Week 15, the participants answered the listening parts of the TOEIC®. Although this test was identical to that of Week 1, the participants were not provided with the answers of the initial test and were not informed that the same test would be used in Week 15. This guaranteed the test's validity and allowed us to compare the scores obtained in Weeks 1 and 15.

3.3 Results

The effectiveness of the two types of teaching methods (i.e. dictation training and listening strategy training) for intermediate listeners in EFL listening were investigated. The data concerning the differences for the three groups (i.e. the CG, DTG and LSTG) between Weeks 1 and 15 on the listening parts of the TOEIC® are presented, which is followed by an analysis and a discussion of the data. After the discussion of the effectiveness of these two teaching methods, more detailed observations that focus on both low- and upper-intermediate listeners are made.

First, a two-way ANOVA was employed with two factors, i.e. 'teaching methods' (for the CG, DTG and LSTG) and 'before and after Study I'. Figure 3.1 presents the relative values of the CG, DTG and LSTG scores by comparing Weeks 1 and 15. A quick look at Figure 3.1 shows sharp rises in both the DTG and LSTG.

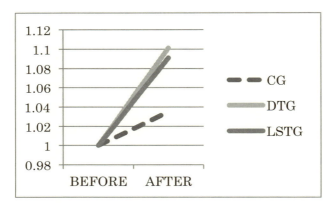

Figure 3.1 Relative values of the CG, DTG and LSTG scores by comparing Weeks 1 and 15 of Study I

Table 3.4 summarises the means, SDs and relative values of these three groups in Weeks 1 and 15.

Table 3.4 Numbers, Means, SDs, Relative Values and Means of Difference of the CG, DTG and LSTG in Weeks 1 and 15 of Study I

	Week 1			Week 15			
	N	*Mean*	*SD*	*Mean*	*SD*	*Relative Value*	*Mean of difference*
CG	10	214.50	41.66	220.00	48.59	1.03	5.50
DTG	52	230.19	28.90	253.46	37.02	1.10	23.27
LSTG	46	241.30	32.41	263.26	45.19	1.09	21.96

Table 3.5 shows the results of the two-way ANOVA and Ryan's method conducted in accordance with the null hypothesis (Table 3.6). The findings show that dictation training is more effective than listening strategy training and that both training methods are significantly effective for intermediate listeners.

Table 3.5 Results of the Two-way ANOVA in Study I

Source	SS	df	MS	F	p
A: Teaching Methods	27532.55	2	13766.27	6.52	0.00 ***
Error[S(A)]	221809.8	105	2112.47		
B: Before & After	9126.42	1	9126.42	14.36	0.00 ****
AB	2086.57	2	1043.28	1.64	0.2
Error[BS(A)]	66720.32	105	635.43		

$+p<.10$, $*p<.05$, $**p<.01$, $***p<.005$, $****p<.001$

Table 3.6 Results of Ryan's Method in Study I

	CG	DTG	LSTG
mean :	217.25	241.83	252.28
n :	20	104	92

pair	r	nominal level	t	p	sig.
LSTG–CG	3	0.02	3.09	0.00	s.
LSTG–DTG	2	0.03	1.59	0.11	n.s.
DTG–CG	2	0.03	2.19	0.03	s.

$MSe = 2112.47$, $df = 105$, significance level $= 0.05$

The effect size of Factor A (teaching methods), Factor B (before and after the study) and the interaction between Factors A and B are medium, small and none, respectively (Table 3.7).

Table 3.7   Effect Sizes in Study I

η_2 in Factor A (Teaching Methods)	0.41
η_2 in Factor B (Before and After)	0.14
η_2 in Interaction of Factors A and B	0.03

Effect Size (r): small = 0.10, medium = 0.30 and large = 0.50

A quick look at Figure 3.2 shows that there are no regular patterns.

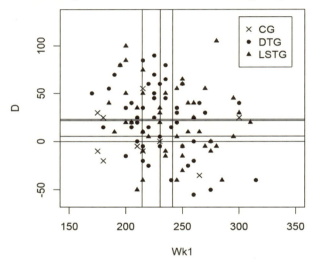

Figure 3.2   Scatter plot of Study I

In the DTG, there were 52 participants of which 37 (71%) increased their scores, 12 (23%) decreased their scores and three (6%) showed no change in Week 15 (Figure 3.3).

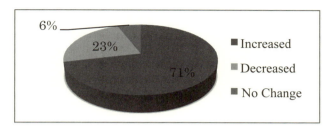

Figure 3.3   Percentage of the DTG participants' score change in Week 15 of Study I

In the DTG, 37 of the 52 participants increased their scores in Week 15 and 32 of these 37 participants (86%) scored less than 250, whereas five (14%) scored 250 or more in Week 1 (Figure 3.4).

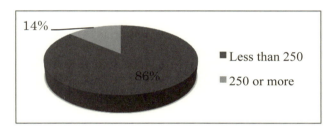

Figure 3.4   Score proportion in Week 1 of the DTG participants whose scores increased in Week 15 of Study I

Another two-way ANOVA was conducted for further investigation on the effect of dictation training between low- and upper-intermediate listeners based on their scores of the listening parts of the TOEIC® in Week 1. There are 39 upper- and 13 low-intermediate listeners in the DTG. The results show that there was significance in the interaction between these two groups at the 1% level (Table 3.8).

Table 3.8   Results of the Two-way ANOVA on the Effect of Dictation Training between Low- and Upper-Intermediate Listeners in Study I

Source	SS	df	MS	F	p
A: More & Less than 250[S(A)]	25308.01	1	25308.01	23.03	0.00 ****
Error[S(A)]	54944.87	50	1098.9		
B: Before & After	4692.63	1	4692.63	8.52	0.01 **
AB	4692.63	1	4692.63	8.52	0.01 **
Error[BS(A)]	27529.49	50	550.59		

$+p < .10$, $*p < .05$, $**p < .01$, $***p < .005$, $****p < .001$

Thus, means for the interaction between 'low- /upper-intermediate listeners' and 'before/after the study' as well as the simple main effect of the interaction between Factors A and B were calculated. The results show that there was significance on the effect of dictation training for low-intermediate listeners at the 0.1% level (Tables 3.9 and 3.10).

Table 3.9   Means of the Interaction between Factors A (Low- and Upper-Intermediate Listeners) and B (before/after the Study) in the DTG of Study I

```
[ Factor A = 1 ] (Upper-Intermediate Listeners)
B ->        1              2
mean :    268.85         268.85
  n :       13             13

[ Factor A = 2 ] (Low-Intermediate Listeners)
B ->        1              2
mean :    217.31         248.33
  n :       39             39
```

Study I - Dictation Training and Listening Strategy Training

Table 3.10 **Simple Main Effect Test of Dictation Training between Low- and Upper-Intermediate Listeners in Study I**

Effect	SS	df	MS	F	p
A(b1)	25898.08	1	25898.08	31.4	0.00 ****
A(b2)	4102.56	1	4102.56	4.97	0.03*
Error	100.00	825			
B(a1)	0.00	1	0.00	0.00	1.00
B(a2)	9385.26	1	9385.26	17.05	0.00 ****
Error	50.00	551			

$+p < .10$, $*p < .05$, $**p < .01$, $***p < .005$, $****p < .001$

In contrast, in the LSTG, there were 46 participants of which 32 (70%) increased their scores, 13 participants (28%) decreased their scores and one participant (2%) showed no change in Week 15 (Figure 3.5).

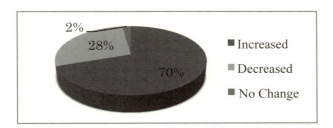

Figure 3.5 **Percentage of the LSTG participants' score change in Week 15 of Study I**

In the LSTG, 32 of the 46 participants increased their scores in Week 15, as mentioned earlier (Figure 3.5), and 19 of these 32 participants (59%) were low-intermediate listeners, whilst 13 participants (41%) were upper-intermediate listeners (Figure 3.6).

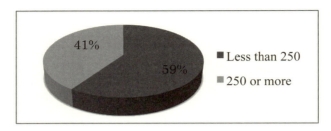

Figure 3.6   Score proportion in Week 1 of the LSTG participants whose scores increased in Week 15 of Study I

Another two-way ANOVA was conducted for further investigation on the effect of listening strategy training between low- and upper-intermediate listeners based on their scores on the listening parts of the TOEIC® in Week 1. There are 25 upper- and 21 low-intermediate listeners in the LSTG. However, there was no significance on the interaction of 'the scores in Week 1' and 'before/after the study' (Table 3.11).

Table 3.11   Results of the Two-way ANOVA on the Effect of Listening Strategy Training between Low- and Upper-Intermediate Listeners in Study I

Source	SS	df	MS	F	p
A: More & Less than 250[S(A)]	59370.65	1	59370.65	53.67	0.00 ****
Error[S(A)]	48675	44	1106.25		
B: Before & After	10772.18	1	10772.18	15.30	0.00 ****
AB	163.48	1	163.48	0.23	0.63
Error[BS(A)]	30973.48	44	703.94		

$+p < .10$, $*p < .05$, $**p < .01$, $***p < .005$, $****p < .001$

Although the majority of the participants in both the DTG (71%) and LSTG (70%) improved their scores in Week 15 (Figures 3.3 and 3.5), it was also observed that many participants in both groups decreased their scores in

Week 15. For example, in the DTG, 12 participants decreased their scores in Week 15, and six of these 12 participants (50%) were low-intermediate listeners (Figure 3.7).

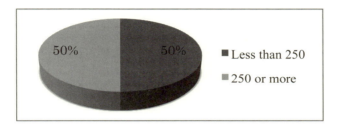

Figure 3.7 Score proportion in Week 1 of the DTG participants whose scores decreased in Week 15 of Study I

On the other hand, in the LSTG, 13 participants decreased their scores in Week 15, and six of these 13 participants (46%) were low-intermediate listeners, whereas seven of these 13 participants (54%) were upper-intermediate listeners (Figure 3.8).

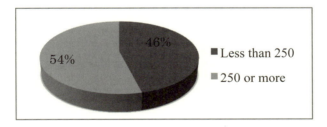

Figure 3.8 Score proportion in Week 1 of the LSTG participants whose scores decreased in Week 15 of Study I

3.4 Discussion

The results illustrated in the aforementioned figures and tables are discussed in the following order:

1. Pre- and post-data for the CG, DTG and LSTG
2. Two-way ANOVA, multiple comparison, effect size and scatter plot
3. The DTG and LSTG participants whose scores increased in Week 15
4. The DTG and LSTG participants whose scores decreased in Week 15

3.4.1 Discussion about the pre- and post-data for the CG, DTG and LSTG

Although the participants of the CG only received regular lessons for 13 weeks, there was some improvement in listening comprehension (Figure 3.1). This confirms that listening comprehension could possibly improve without any particular training, though the level of improvement is not prominent and the process is significantly time consuming. Conversely, both the DTG and LSTG showed sharp increases, thus demonstrating that both dictation training and listening strategy training are effective for intermediate listeners under certain conditions (in this case, 30 minutes a week for 13 weeks).

As shown above in Table 3.4, in Week 1, the mean scores of the CG, DTG and LSTG were 214.50, 230.19 and 241.30, respectively, whereas in Week 15, the mean scores were 220.00, 253.46 and 263.26, respectively. To compare these data as the relative values, the mean scores of each group in Week 1 were treated as 1.00 and compared with those in Week 15. The relative values of the CG, DTG and LSTG were 1.03, 1.10 and 1.09, respectively. The LSTG had the highest mean score in Week 1, but the most prominent improvement was observed in the DTG. This indicates that dictation training may be more suitable than listening strategy training for intermediate learners. If so, this assumption does not contradict the theories of both Schneider and Shiffrin (1977) and Anderson (2010). There are

Study I - Dictation Training and Listening Strategy Training

gradual steps in both human information processing and language learning. Nation and Newton (2009) also support the importance of bottom-up processes such as dictation training in listening: 'learners need to be proficient with these bottom-up processes and...learners can benefit from being taught how to listen' (p. 41). The following section analyses the data from a different perspective.

3.4.2 Discussion about the two-way ANOVA, multiple comparison, effect size and scatter plot

A two-way ANOVA was conducted on two factors (i.e. teaching methods and before/after the study) and significance was observed in both these factors, as shown in Table 3.5. There was significance in 'teaching methods' at the 0.5% level and 'before and after the study' at the 0.1% level. Thus, Ryan's method, which is one of the multiple comparison methods, was utilised for further analysis. The results reveal significance between the CG and DTG as well as between the CG and LSTG, though no significance was found between the DTG and LSTG (Table 3.6). Note that listening strategy training is *also* significantly effective after dictation training for intermediate listeners. The results of Study I are supported by other researchers such as Graham et al. (2008), Vogley (1995), Vandergrift (1997; 1998) and Baleghizadeh and Rahimi (2011) who claim that strategy development seems to be related to proficiency issues.

The effect size of Study I also supports the finding that both teaching methods (i.e. dictation training and listening strategy training) are significantly effective for intermediate listeners. When deciding whether a study is significant, a p value is usually employed at the 5% level. However, the larger the sample size, the smaller the p value, which suggests that p value changes depend on sample size, and it provides no substantial information regarding whether a difference exists. Mizumoto and Takeuchi (2011) claim that a p value should not be the only data used for significance but the mean, SD and effect size should also be reported (p. 49). Other researchers claim that regardless of significance, effect size should be reported, since there are both cases of 'significance with a small effect size' and 'no significance with a large effect size' (Kline, 2004; American Psychology Association, 2001; Field, 2009). Therefore, effect size, which does not change depending on the sample size, is used in this study. Furthermore, effect size is categorised into three groups (i.e. small, medium and large), and the numerical value varies depending on the type of statistical analysis. According to Mizumoto and Takeuchi (2011, p. 51), the numerical values of effect size include: 0.10 (small), 0.30 (medium) and 0.50 (large) for both a one- and two-way ANOVA. In Study I, the effect size of the teaching methods was 0.41 (i.e. between medium and large), which signifies that both dictation training and listening strategy training are significantly effective (Table 3.7).

The effect of dictation training, especially for less-proficient listeners, is supported by numerous researchers such as Oller (1971), Kakehi et al. (1981), Suenobu et al. (1982), Morris (1983), Itakura et al. (1985), Ito (1990), Nishino (1992), Fujinaga (2002), Wilson (2003), Watanabe (2009) and Satori (2010). Yonezaki (2014) emphasises the effectiveness of dictation, especially for Japanese learners, as follows: Most Japanese learners of English have problems in perception, which is vital for bottom-up processing, and due to such problems, they are unable to activate syntactic knowledge and background knowledge (p. 2). Conversely, there are some ambiguities in the research results. For example, Nishino's study (1992) with 84 university students report that vocabulary is critical and that background knowledge and speech perception are good predictors of listening comprehension. However, no standardised test was used to determine the comprehension level of the participants prior to the study. Thus, the results are inconclusive.

Furthermore, Watanabe (2009) investigates the effects of dictation practice on the TOEIC® listening parts with 82 Japanese college students and found that a larger quantity of dictation tends to have a greater effect than a smaller amount. However, both the pre- and post-scores of the participants are not shown. Therefore, it is unclear for which comprehension level dictation practice was proved effective. In addition, she does not describe how the participants were assessed on dictation. As Buck (2001, p. 75) indicates, there are numerous ways to score dictations. Hughes (1989) also suggests that scoring for low-ability test takers can be extremely difficult when they make many mistakes since it is not always clear which parts of the texts their responses are referring to. Without mentioning the comprehension level of the participants and how they are assessed on dictation, these research results remain ambiguous.

Since listening strategy training is also effective, it could be considered that intermediate listeners are capable of employing listening strategies to some extent even though their perception level has not been fully automatised. Buck (2001) states that listening comprehension is the result of an interaction between numerous information sources, such as acoustic input, different types of linguistic knowledge, details of the context and general world knowledge, and listeners use whatever information they have available to help them interpret what the speaker is saying (p. 3). Therefore, they can maintain a certain capacity for some instructed listening strategies. This assumption is supported by the effect size of Factor B ('before and after the study'), which is 0.14 (between small and medium). These results indicate that there is effectiveness in both 'teaching methods' and 'before and after the study'.

Next, a closer examination of the scatter plot reveals that there is no regular pattern and that even some CG participants increased their scores, whereas many DTG and LSTG participants decreased their scores in Week 15 (Figure 3.2). Based on these findings, it is assumed that the score range between 166 and 330 in the listening parts of the TOEIC® as 'intermediate' is possibly very wide to induce any type of pattern or tendency. Thus, for further analysis, the score range of 166–330 was sub-divided into two ranges, i.e. 166–249 as low-intermediate and 250–330 as upper-intermediate.

3.4.3 Discussion about the DTG and LSTG participants whose scores increased in Week 15

First, let us observe those participants in the DTG who increased their scores in Week 15. As shown in Figure 3.3, 37 out of 52 participants (71%) in the DTG increased their scores in Week 15, and amongst them, 86% (32 out of 37) were low-intermediate listeners (Figure 3.4). Then, for a further analysis, a two-way ANOVA was conducted on two factors, i.e. 'more/less than 250 in Week 1' and 'before/after the study'. The results show that there was significance in the interaction between these two factors at the 1% level, as shown in Table 3.8. The simple main effect test about the effect of dictation training also shows significance between the 13 upper- and 39 low-intermediate listeners based on their scores of the listening parts of the TOEIC® in Week 1 (Table 3.9). These results indicate that dictation training is significantly effective, especially for low-intermediate listeners at the 0.1% level (Table 3.10).

Similarly, the same feature is also observed in the LSTG. As shown in Figure 3.5, 32 out of 46 participants (70%) in the LSTG increased their scores in Week 15, and amongst them, 59% (19 out of 32) were low-intermediate listeners (Figure 3.6). Again, a two-way ANOVA was conducted for further analysis on two factors, i.e. 'more/less than 250 in Week 1' and 'before/after the study'.

However, no significance was observed in the interaction between these two elements on listening strategy training. The possible reason for this is that the TOEIC® listening score of 250 might be a borderline of perception, following Anderson's (2010) theory. When a participant's score is less than 250 in the listening parts of the TOEIC®, these low-intermediate listeners will most probably remain at the lowest level, i.e. perception, according to Anderson's theory (2010) and also persist in controlled processing, following the theory of Schneider and Shiffrin (1977). Thus, specific training, such as listening strategy training (which requires more capacity for automatic processing), is not as effective as dictation training,

Study I - Dictation Training and Listening Strategy Training

which focuses on phonetic level. To employ instructed listening strategy effectively, these participants need to reach the level where perception is fully automatised. This assumption correlates with the theories of Schneider and Shiffrin (1977) and Anderson (2010).

As shown in Figure 3.4, 14% (5 out of 37) of the DTG upper-intermediate participants might have overcome the level of perception. Thus, basic phonetic perception training, such as dictation training, might be less effective for those who have passed the level of perception. This assumption is also supported by the data of the LSTG. When comparing the score portions in Week 1 of both the DTG and LSTG participants whose scores increased in Week 15, 86% (32 out of 370) of the DTG increased their scores, whereas only 59% (19 out of 32) of the LSTG increased their scores (Figure 3.6). This result might be considered as evidence of what Schneider and Shiffrin (1977) and Anderson (2010) claim in their theories: Human information processing and language acquisition involve gradual steps. Moreover, according to Schneider and Shiffrin's (1977) theory, low-intermediate listeners might not have passed the stage of controlled processing. As per Anderson's (2010) theory, they might remain at the lowest level, i.e. perception.

Finally, unless phonetic perception is automatically processed, there is almost no capacity to activate adequate listening strategies for listening tasks. As a result, low-intermediate listeners still considerably remain in controlled processing, and they still have to primarily focus on incoming phonetic information during the perception stage. Therefore, the greater the capacity used for perception and parsing in a single listening activity, the less capacity is available for comprehension itself. As previously discussed in the theory of Anderson (2010), when perception requires more time and cognitive burden, comprehension suffers. Considering the use of listening strategies compared to dictation in terms of information processing, perception must be automatically processed so that there is a greater capacity to activate adequate listening strategies that depend on particular listening tasks.

Therefore, listening strategy training might not be as effective as dictation training for low-intermediate listeners. These results indicate the complexity of the elements and factors related to improving EFL/ESL listening comprehension.

3.4.4 Discussion about the DTG and LSTG participants whose scores decreased in Week 15

In Study I, both dictation training and listening strategy training were significantly effective for intermediate listeners under a certain condition in which training was provided 30 minutes a week for 13 weeks. Whilst the majority of the participants in both groups increased their scores in Week 15, many participants in both groups also decreased their scores in Week 15.

First, let us observe the DTG. As shown in Figure 3.3, 23% (12 out of 52) of the DTG participants decreased their scores in Week 15, and amongst them, 50% (6 out of 12) were upper-intermediate listeners. A comparison of Figures 3.4 and 3.7 suggests that when receiving a 30-minute dictation training once a week for 13 weeks, upper-intermediate listeners are more likely to decrease their scores. One possible reason for this could be explained with the score of 250 in the listening parts of the TOEIC®. Those participants who achieved TOEIC® listening scores of 250 or more in Week 1 might have overcome the level of perception, and this assumption is also supported by the various data of the DTG. For example, in the DTG, 6% of the participants (3 out of 52) showed no change in their scores in Weeks 1 and 15 (Figure 3.3). In fact, their scores were 210, 260 and 275 (Appendix D). Apart from one participant, the other two scores were more than 250. For upper-intermediate listeners, basic phonetic perception training, such as dictation training, might be less effective since the majority of them have already passed the level of perception. Thus, dictation training might be less effective for upper-intermediate listeners. This assumption and the results are consistent with the theories of Schneider and Shiffrin (1977) and Anderson (2010).

On the other hand, for the LSTG, Figure 3.5 shows that 28% (13 out of 46) of the LSTG participants decreased their scores in Week 15, and amongst them, 54% (seven out of 13) were upper-intermediate listeners (Figure 3.8). In both the DTG (50%) and LSTG (54%), approximately half of those who decreased their scores in Week 15 were upper-intermediate listeners (Figures 3.7 and 3.8). A comparison of Figures 3.6 and 3.8 implies that when receiving a 30-minute listening strategy training once a week for 13 weeks, upper-intermediate listeners are more likely to decrease their scores. As proven so far, if those participants who achieved TOEIC® listening scores of 250 or more in Week 1 might have overcome the level of perception, then theoretically speaking, listening strategy training could be specifically effective for upper-intermediate listeners. Although listening strategy training was significantly effective for the intermediate listeners in this study, its significance was not observed between the low- and upper-intermediate listeners, which is not consistent with the theories of Schneider and Shiffrin (1977) and Anderson (2010).

One possible reason for this is that there is a limitation to assuming and explaining this result based only on the TOEIC® listening score of 250. The complexity of the elements and factors related to improving EFL/ESL listening comprehension must be clarified through a deeper investigation. Therefore, the MALQ is employed for further analysis of the elements in Studies II and III.

3.5 Summary

S-1 Both dictation training and listening strategy training are significantly effective for intermediate listeners.

S-2 Dictation training is significantly effective, especially for low-intermediate listeners.

A total of 108 Japanese learners of English participated in Study I. Only those who scored between 166 and 330 in the listening parts of the TOEIC® in Week 1 were selected after which they were divided into three groups, i.e. the CG (10), DTG (52) and LSTG (46). During Weeks 2 and 14, the CG participants had no training other than their usual 90-minute class each week. The DTG participants received dictation training for 30 minutes in their usual 90-minute class each week, whereas the LSTG participants were taught the various types of listening strategies for 30 minutes in their 90-minute class each week. In Week 15, all the participants took the same listening parts of the TOEIC® as in Week 1.

The results show that 71% of the DTG participants and 70% of the LSTG participants increased their scores in Week 15 and that significance was observed in their increases of both the DTG and LSTG with a two-way ANOVA. Based on the idea that the score range from 166 to 330 in the listening parts of the TOEIC® is probably very broad to obtain a concrete result, the DTG and LSTG participants were further divided into two groups, i.e. low-intermediate listeners (who scored less than 250 in the listening parts of the TOEIC® in Week 1) and upper-intermediate listeners (who scored 250 or more in the listening parts of the TOEIC® in Week 1). In addition, the results of a two-way ANOVA show that, in the DTG, there was significant effectiveness of dictation training, especially for low-intermediate listeners. However, no significance was obtained between 'low- and upper-intermediate listeners' and 'listening strategy training' in the LSTG.

Chapter 4: Study II—Combined Training with the MALQ

4.1 Hypotheses

As stated in Chapter 3, both dictation training and listening strategy training were significantly effective for the Japanese EFL intermediate listeners in Study I. In addition, dictation training was significantly effective specifically for the lower-intermediate listeners who scored less than 250 in the listening parts of the TOEIC® in Week 1. When the results of Study I were presented at the 48th Annual Meeting of the British Association of Applied Linguistics in Southampton, England in 2012, Professor Suzanne Graham from Reading University suggested investigating the synergistic effect of both dictation training and listening strategy training. What is assumed, based on the theories of Schneider and Shiffrin (1977) and Anderson (2010), is that there are gradual steps in both human information processing and language acquisition. Due to the limited capability of information processing and language acquisition at the level of intermediate listeners, it does not allow them to select the best listening strategy or automatically combine multiple listening strategies whilst simultaneously dealing with perception. In fact, applying both approaches simultaneously would be extremely demanding for intermediate listeners since basic skills, such as perception, have not fully reached the automatic processing. Therefore, Study II posits the following hypothesis:

H-1 For intermediate listeners, the combined training of dictation and listening strategy is not effective for improving EFL listening comprehension.

Next, as stated in Chapter 2, metacognitive knowledge and its usage is the key to becoming a successful listener. In Study II, the MALQ was used to investigate how the metacognitive awareness of the participants changes before and after the study. Although significance in the effectiveness of dictation training and listening strategy training was obtained in Study I, these two types of training were provided separately for two different groups of listeners.

In Study II, both dictation training and listening strategy training were combined and instructed to one group. As stated earlier, combined training can be too much information for intermediate listeners to process since they do not have enough capacity for the usage of metacognitive awareness; they could neither plan, monitor nor evaluate their comprehension sufficiently. Even though they could become aware of the importance of metacognitive awareness in EFL listening and acquire a certain degree of metacognitive knowledge through this combined training, they would not fully employ it whilst listening since basic skills, such as perception and parsing, have not reached the automatic processing.

4.2 Method
4.2.1 Participants

The participants in Study II consisted of 57 first-year students (in the Faculty of Economics) at a Japanese private university who obtained the TOEIC® listening scores between 166 and 330 in April 2013. The same listening parts of the TOEIC® as in Study I were used to select the participants of Study II. The participants received four 90-minute English lessons per week in reading, writing, listening and computer-assisted language learning. Initially, there were more participants, but only those who attended all 15 classes between April and July 2013 were chosen for Study II. The participants were divided into two groups, i.e. 28 in the CG, with half of them belonging to the EFL reading class and the other half belonging to another EFL reading class and 29 in the dictation and listening strategy training group (D+LSTG), with half of them belonging to the general EFL class and the other half belonging to the English presentation class. All the lessons were presented in English as per the policy of the faculty. All the classes were part of the regular English curriculum, and none of the participants' major subject was English. Table 4.1 summarises the means, SDs and relative values of these two groups in Week 1.

Table 4.1 Numbers, Means and SDs of the CG and D+LSTG in Week 1 of Study II

Group	N	Mean	SD
CG	28	246.96	32.58
D+LSTG	29	257.24	39.29

4.2.2 Materials

With the same materials as Study I, the MALQ was used for further analysis in Study II in addition to the scores of the listening parts of the TOEIC®. As introduced in Chapter 2, the MALQ is a questionnaire with 21 questions designed by Vandergrift, Goh, Mareschal and Tafaghodtari in 2006 for researchers and instructors to assess the extent to which language learners are aware of and can regulate the process of second language (L2) listening comprehension. It is also intended to serve as a self-assessment instrument in which learners can evaluate their awareness of the listening process and reflect on their strategy use when listening to L2 texts (p. 432).

The 21 questions were categorised into five groups (Table 4.2):

1) Problem solving (guessing as well as monitoring these guesses)
2) Planning/evaluation (preparing to listen and assessing success)
3) Mental translation (translation from English to L1 when listening)
4) Person knowledge (confidence or anxiety and self-perception as a listener)
5) Directed attention (ways of concentrating on certain aspects of a task)

Table 4.2   Categories of Each Question in the MALQ

Question No.	Categories	Question No.	Categories
1	Planning/evaluation	11	Mental translation
2	Directed attention	12	Directed attention
3	Person knowledge	13	Problem-solving
4	Mental translation	14	Planning/evaluation
5	Problem-solving	15	Person knowledge
6	Directed attention	16	Directed attention
7	Problem-solving	17	Problem-solving
8	Person knowledge	18	Mental translation
9	Problem-solving	19	Problem-solving
10	Planning/evaluation	20	Planning/evaluation
		21	Planning/evaluation

To prevent the participants from realising the purpose of each question, none of these categories are printed in the MALQ. The original MALQ is written in English, but the Japanese translation was added underneath each question to avoid any misunderstandings. Each question includes six scales (Table 4.3): 1 = Strongly disagree, 2 = Disagree, 3 = Slightly disagree, 4 = Partly agree, 5 = Agree and 6 = Strongly agree. For a full reference of the MALQ, see Appendix F.

Table 4.3   Excerpt of the MALQ

Strongly disagree	Disagree	Slightly disagree	Partly agree	Agree	Strongly agree
全く違う	反対	どちらかと いうと反対	どちらかと いうと賛成	賛成	全くその通り
1	2	3	4	5	6

1. Before I start to listen, I have a plan in my head for how I am going to listen.
   聞く前に、どのようにして聞くのか頭の中でプランを立てる。   1 2 3 4 5 6

2. I focus harder on the text when I have trouble understanding.   1 2 3 4 5 6
   わからなくなった時は、内容により集中する。

3. I find that listening is more difficult than reading, speaking, or writing in English.
   リーディングやスピーキング、ライティングよりも、リスニングが一番難しい。   1 2 3 4 5 6

4.2.3 Procedure

The same materials and procedures in Study I were used for Study II. For the CG, the listening parts of the TOEIC® and MALQ were administered in Week 1 to select the participants and determine their metacognitive awareness in EFL listening before the study. The participants in the CG received lessons based on the class textbook from Weeks 2 to 14. Furthermore, for credibility, the same listening parts of the TOEIC® and MALQ were administered in Week 15. However, the answers of the initial test were not provided, and none of the participants were informed of this procedure at all.

For the D+LSTG, the same listening parts of the TOEIC® were also administered in Week 1 to select the participants for Study II. From Weeks 2 to 14, a combined 60-minute training (both dictation training and listening strategy training for 30 minutes each, with instructions in Japanese) with the same materials from Study I was conducted during the 90-minute lessons and for the remaining 30 minutes, they received lessons based on the class textbook for 13 weeks. In Study II, dictation training was provided prior to listening strategy training and following procedure (the same as Study I) was employed.

In Step 1, the D+LSTG participants were first informed about the purpose and subject of the training after which they listened to the relevant parts of the CD (attached to the textbook) only once. Whilst listening, they dictated some words/phrases/short sentences on the provided handouts, which the present author had created based on the textbook's exercise page. Then, the answers were provided.

In Step 2, the participants viewed the answers whilst listening to the CD for second time to combine the written words/phrases/short sentences that they could not dictate *with* the acoustic information.

In Step 3, the participants listened to the CD a third time *without* looking at the answers to comprehend the words/phrases/short sentences that they were unable to dictate purely through the acoustic information.

Next, listening strategy training was provided. The participants were first instructed on the logical aspects of the relevant listening strategies for that lesson. Then, they performed listening tasks that involved applying the presented listening strategies, after which they were provided with the answers and pertinent feedback.

In Week 15, the participants answered both the listening parts of the TOEIC® and MALQ. Although this test was identical to that of Week 1, the participants were not provided with the answers of the initial test and were not informed that the same test would be used in Week 15. This guaranteed the test's validity and allowed a comparison of the scores obtained in Weeks 1 and 15.

4.3 Results

The effectiveness of the combined teaching method of dictation training and listening strategy training for intermediate listeners in EFL listening was investigated. The data concerning the differences for the two groups (i.e. CG and D+LSTG) between Weeks 1 and 15 on the listening parts of the TOEIC® are presented, which is followed by an analysis and discussion of the data. After the discussion of the effectiveness of the combined teaching method, more detailed observations that focus on both low- and upper-intermediate listeners and the differences in the MALQ before and after the study are discussed.

First, a two-way ANOVA was employed with two factors, i.e. 'teaching methods' (for the CG and D+ LSTG) and 'before and after Study II'. Figure 4.1 presents the relative values of the CG and D+LSTG scores by comparing Weeks 1 and 15. Table 4.4 summarises the means, SDs and relative values of these two groups in Weeks 1 and 15. A quick look at Figure 4.1 shows almost an identical sharp rise in both the CG and D+LSTG.

Study II - Combined Training with the MALQ

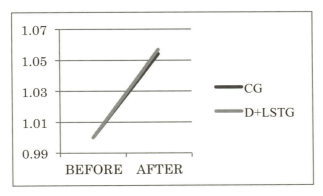

Figure 4.1 Relative values of the CG and D+LSTG scores by comparing Weeks 1 and 15 of Study I

Table 4.4 Numbers, Means, SDs, Relative Values and Means of Difference of the CG and D+LSTG in Weeks 1 and 15 of Study I

	Week 1			Week 15			
	N	Mean	SD	Mean	SD	Relative Value	Mean of difference
CG	28	246.96	32.58	260.36	39.49	1.05	13.40
D+LSTG	29	257.24	39.29	271.90	39.94	1.06	14.66

Table 4.5 shows the results of a two-way ANOVA conducted in accordance with the null hypothesis. The findings show that the combined teaching method is not significantly effective for intermediate listeners.

Table 4.5 Results of the Two-way ANOVA in Study II

Source	SS	df	MS	F	p
A: Teaching Method	3390.17	1	3390.17	1.41	0.24
Error[S(A)]	132688.8	55	2412.52		
B: Before & After	5603.46	1	5603.46	11.87	0.00 ***
AB	11.35	1	11.35	0.02	0.88
Error[BS(A)]	25974.62	55	472.27		

$+ p<.10, * p<.05, ** p<.01, *** p<.005, **** p<.001$

The effect size of Factor A (teaching method), Factor B (before/after) and the interaction between Factors A and B in Study II are small, small and none, respectively (Table 4.6).

Table 4.6 Effect Sizes in Study II

$\eta 2$ in Factor A (Teaching Method)	0.13
$\eta 2$ in Factor A (Before and After)	0.22
$\eta 2$ in Interaction of Factors A and B	0.00

Effect Size (r): small = 0.10, medium = 0.30, large = 0.50

A quick look at Figure 4.2 shows that there are no regular patterns.

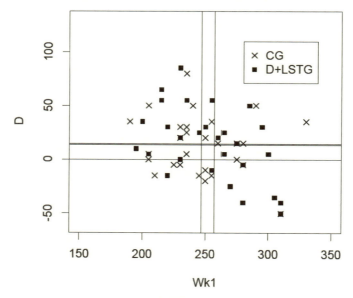

Figure 4.2 Scatter plot of Study II

In the D+LSTG, there were 29 participants of which 20 (69%) increased their scores, eight (28%) decreased their scores and one (3%) showed no change in Week 15 (Figure 4.3).

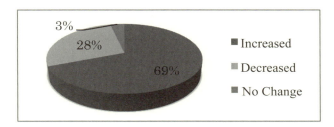

Figure 4.3   Percentage of the D+LSTG participants' score change in Week 15 of Study II

In the D+LSTG, 20 of the 29 participants increased their scores in Week 15, and 10 of these 20 participants (50%) were low-intermediate listeners (Figure 4.4).

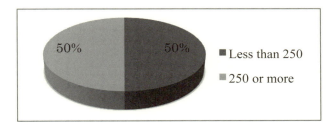

Figure 4.4   Score proportion in Week 1 of the D+LSTG participants whose scores increased in Week 15 of Study II

In the D+LSTG, eight participants (28%) decreased their scores in Week 15, and only one of these eight participants (12%) was a low-intermediate listener. The other seven participants (88%) were

75

upper-intermediate listeners (Figure 4.5).

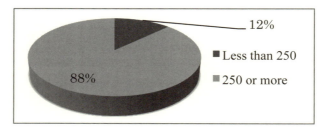

Figure 4.5 Score proportion in Week 1 of the D+LSTG participants whose scores decreased in Week 15 of Study II

Figure 4.6 shows the pre- and post-mean scores of the CG on the MLAQ in Study II.

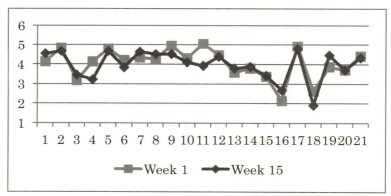

Figure 4.6 Pre- and post-mean scores of the CG on the MALQ in Study II

Table 4.7 shows a summary of the changes regarding the metacognitive awareness of the CG participants before and after the study. A closer look at the table shows that Nos. 15 and 20 show no change, the mean scale scores of Nos. 1, 3, 7, 8, 13, 14, 16 and 19 increased and that the others

76

decreased after the study.

Table 4.7 Pre- and Post-Mean Scores of the CG on the MALQ in Study II

CG	1	2	3	4	5	6	7	8	9	10	11	12	13	14	15	16	17	18	19	20	21
Wk 1	4.1	4.8	3.2	4.1	4.8	4.2	4.3	4.3	5	4.3	5	4.5	3.6	3.8	3.4	2.1	4.9	2.6	3.9	3.7	4.4
Wk 15	4.5	4.7	3.5	3.2	4.7	3.8	4.6	4.5	4.5	4.1	3.9	4.4	3.8	3.9	3.4	2.7	4.8	1.9	4.5	3.7	4.3
D	0.4	-0.1	0.3	-0.9	-0.1	-0.4	0.3	0.2	-0.5	-0.2	-1.1	-0.1	0.2	0.1	0	0.6	-0.1	-0.7	0.6	0	-0.1

Figure 4.7 presents the pre- and post-mean scores of the D+LSTG on the MALQ in Study II.

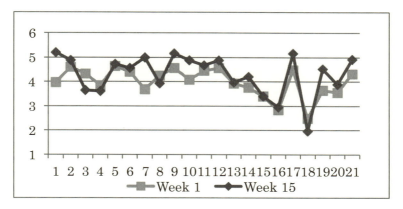

Figure 4.7 Pre- and post-mean scores of the D+LSTG on the MALQ in Study II

Table 4.8 shows a summary of the changes regarding the metacognitive awareness of the D+LSTG participants before and after the study. A closer look at the table shows that No. 15 showed no change, the mean scale scores of Nos. 3, 4, 8 and 18 decreased and that the others increased after the study.

77

Table 4.8 Pre- and Post-Mean Scores of the D+LSTG on the MALQ in Study II

D+LSTG	1	2	3	4	5	6	7	8	9	10	11	12	13	14	15	16	17	18	19	20	21
Wk 1	4	4.6	4.3	3.8	4.6	4.4	3.7	4.2	4.6	4.1	4.4	4.6	3.9	3.8	3.4	2.8	4.5	2.5	3.6	3.6	4.3
Wk 15	5.2	4.9	3.6	3.6	4.7	4.6	5	3.9	5.2	4.9	4.7	4.9	4	4.2	3.4	3	5.2	2	4.5	3.9	4.9
D	1.2	0.3	-0.7	-0.2	0.1	0.2	1.3	-0.3	0.6	0.8	0.3	0.3	0.1	0.4	0	0.2	0.7	-0.5	0.9	0.3	0.6

Next, for further analysis on metacognitive awareness before and after the study, the D+LSTG participants were divided into two categories, i.e. the top 11 participants who increased their scores and the bottom eight participants who decreased their scores in Week 15. For more details of these participants, see Tables 4.9 and 4.10.

Table 4.9 Scores of the Top 11 D+LSTG Participants whose Scores Increased in Week 15 of Study II

Participants	Week 1	Week 15	Difference	Rank
1	230	315	85	1
2	215	280	65	2
3	255	310	55	3
4	235	290	55	3
5	285	335	50	5
6	200	235	35	6
7	250	280	30	7
8	295	325	30	7
9	360	385	25	9
10	265	290	25	9
11	245	270	25	9

Table 4.10   Scores of the Bottom Eight D+LSTG Participants whose Scores Decreased in Week 15 of Study II

Participants	Week 1	Week 15	Difference	Rank
1	310	260	-50	1
2	280	240	-40	2
3	310	270	-40	2
4	305	270	-35	4
5	270	245	-25	5
6	220	205	-15	6
7	255	245	-10	7
8	280	275	-5	8

Figure 4.8 presents the pre- and post-mean scores of the top 11 D+LSTG participants on the MALQ in Study II.

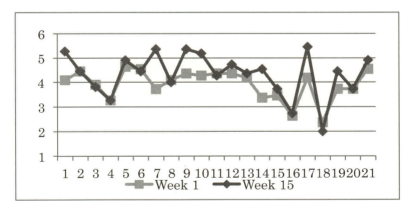

Figure 4.8   Pre- and post-mean scores of the top 11 D+LSTG participants on the MALQ in Study II

Table 4.11 shows a summary of the changes regarding the metacognitive awareness of the top 11 D+LSTG participants before and after the study. A closer look at the table shows that Nos. 2, 4, 6 and 20 showed no change, and the mean scale scores of Nos. 3, 8, 11 and 18 decreased, whereas the others increased after the study.

Table 4.11   Pre- and Post-Mean Scores of the Top 11 D+LSTG Participants whose Scores Increased on the MALQ in Study II

D+LSTG Top 11	1	2	3	4	5	6	7	8	9	10	11	12	13	14	15	16	17	18	19	20	21
Wk 1	4.1	4.5	3.9	3.3	4.6	4.5	3.7	4.1	4.4	4.3	4.4	4.4	4.2	3.4	3.5	2.6	4.2	2.4	3.7	3.7	4.5
Wk 15	5.3	4.5	3.8	3.3	4.9	4.5	5.4	4	5.4	5.2	4.3	4.7	4.4	4.5	3.7	2.7	5.5	2	4.5	3.7	4.9
D	1.2	0	-0.1	0	0.3	0	1.7	-0.1	1.0	0.9	-0.1	0.3	0.2	1.1	0.2	0.1	1.3	-0.4	0.8	0	0.4

Next, Figure 4.9 presents the pre- and post-mean scores of the bottom eight D+LSTG participants on the MALQ in Study II.

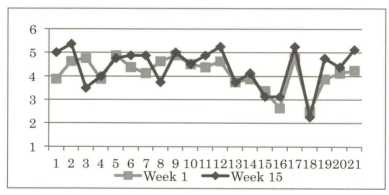

Figure 4.9   Pre- and post-mean scores of the bottom eight D+LSTG participants on the MALQ in Study II

Table 4.12 presents a summary of the changes regarding the metacognitive awareness of the bottom eight D+LSTG participants before and after the study. A closer look at the table shows that Nos. 10 and 13 showed no change, and the mean scale scores of Nos. 3, 5, 8, 15 and 18 decreased, whereas the others increased after the study.

Study II - Combined Training with the MALQ

Table 4.12 Pre- and Post-Mean Scores of the Bottom Eight D+LSTG Participants whose Scores Decreased on the MALQ in Study II

D+LSTG Bottom 8	1	2	3	4	5	6	7	8	9	10	11	12	13	14	15	16	17	18	19	20	21
Wk 1	3.9	4.6	4.8	3.9	4.9	4.4	4.1	4.6	4.9	4.5	4.4	4.6	3.8	3.9	3.4	2.6	4.8	2.5	3.9	4.1	4.3
Wk 15	5	5.4	3.5	4	4.8	4.9	4.9	3.8	5	4.5	4.9	5.3	3.8	4.1	3.1	3.1	5.3	2.3	4.8	4.4	5.1
D	1.1	0.8	-1.3	0.1	-0.1	0.5	0.8	-0.8	0.1	0	0.5	0.7	0	0.2	-0.3	0.5	0.5	-0.2	0.9	0.3	0.8

Table 4.13 displays a summary of the changes regarding metacognitive awareness in the CG and D+LSTG. The D+LSTG are further divided into two groups.

Table 4.13 Summary of the MALQ before and after Study II

Item No.	Categories	CG	D+LSTG	Top 11	Bottom 8
1	Planning/evaluation	△	○	○	○
2	Directed attention	↓	△	—	△
3	Person knowledge	△	↓	↓	↓↓
4	Mental translation	↓	↓	—	△
5	Problem-solving	↓	△	△	↓
6	Directed attention	↓	△	—	△
7	Problem-solving	△	○	○	△
8	Person knowledge	△	↓	↓	↓
9	Problem-solving	↓	△	○	△
10	Planning/evaluation	↓	△	△	—
11	Mental translation	↓↓	△	↓	△
12	Directed attention	↓	△	△	△
13	Problem-solving	△	△	△	—
14	Planning/evaluation	△	△	○	△
15	Person knowledge	—	—	△	↓
16	Directed attention	△	△	△	△
17	Problem-solving	↓	△	○	△
18	Mental translation	↓	↓	↓	↓
19	Problem-solving	△	△	△	△
20	Planning/evaluation	—	△	—	△
21	Planning/evaluation	↓	△	△	△

○: Increased more than 1.0
△: Increased less than 1.0
—: No change
↓: Decreased less than 1.0
↓↓: Decreased over 1.0

4.4 Discussion

The results depicted in figures and tables are discussed in the following order:

1. Pre- and post-data for the CG and D+LSTG
2. Two-way ANOVA, effect size and scatter plot
3. The D+LSTG participants whose scores increased and decreased in Week 15
4. The MALQ

4.4.1 Discussion about the pre- and post-data for the CG and D+LSTG

Although the participants of the CG only received regular lessons for 13 weeks, there was an improvement in listening comprehension in English. The TOEIC® listening scores in Week 15 reflected almost identical increases when compared with the scores of the D+LSTG participants (Figure 4.1). In fact, they actually improved as much as the D+LSTG participants who received dictation training and listening strategy training for 60 minutes a week for 13 weeks.

At this point, let us observe more concrete data. As shown in Table 4.4, the mean scores of the CG and D+LSTG were 246.96 and 257.24, respectively, in Week 1, whilst their mean scores in Week 15 were 260.36 and 271.90, respectively. To compare these data as the relative values, the mean scores of each group in Week 1 were treated as 1.00 and compared with those in Week 15. The relative values of the CG and D+LSTG were 1.05 and 1.06, respectively. This demonstrates that the combined training was not effective for intermediate listeners, though both types of training were effective when they were separately applied, as proven in Chapter 3. Thus, it is assumed that the intermediate learners in Study II may not have fully passed the level of perception or controlled processing, as stipulated in both Anderson's (2010) and Schneider and Shiffrin's (1977) theories.

Although there is no difference between the CG and D+LSTG in Study III, the percentage of those who increased their scores in the D+LSTG in Week 15 of Study II was 69%, which is a similar percentage to Study I. The percentages of those who increased their scores in the DTG and LSTG in Week 15 of Study I was 71% and 70%, respectively. The participants in both Studies I and II might have understood the importance of using the various types of listening strategies *theoretically*. However, since perception was not fully automatised, they probably lacked the capacity to freely deal with listening strategies. As previously observed in regard to listening (based on Anderson's theory), when the capacity used for perception in a single listening activity increases, the available capacity for utilisation decreases. In other words, when perception and parsing require more time and cognitive energy, comprehension is significantly affected. Until intermediate listeners can reach the automatised level regarding perception and parsing, choosing the appropriate listening strategies based on the task would probably be very demanding. Thus, it can be concluded that the majority of the participants in Study II have not reached the level at which a sequence of cognitive activities in English listening comprehension can automatically occur without conscious attention and active control. This result is also consistent with Schneider and Shiffrin's (1977) and Anderson's (2010) theories in which human information processing and language acquisition involve gradual steps.

In the next section, the data is analysed from a different perspective.

4.4.2 Discussion about the two-way ANOVA, effect size and scatter plot

A two-way ANOVA was conducted on two factors, i.e. 'teaching method' and 'before/after Study II'. The results reveal that there was no significance in the teaching method (Table 4.5). Although no significance was observed, this result does not contradict the theories of both Schneider and Shiffrin (1977) and Anderson (2010). As discussed in Study I, both dictation training and listening strategy training are significantly effective when they are separately applied. Since the participants in both Studies I and II had not reached the level of utilisation where perception and parsing automatically occur, it resulted in an almost identical progress of the CG participants. Thus, it is natural to conclude that the participants did not find the combined teaching method beneficial in Study II. For them, having dictation training and listening strategy training provided separately was more manageable.

The effect size of Study II also supports that the combined training is not effective for intermediate listeners. As introduced in Chapter 3, effect size neither changes nor depends on the sample size. In Study II, the effect size of teaching method was 0.13, which means that the effect of the combined teaching method was small (Table 4.6). Furthermore, a closer examination of the scatter plot reveals that there is no regular pattern and that both the CG and D+LSTG participants increased and decreased their scores in Week 15 (Figure 4.2). Based on these findings, it is assumed that the score range from 166 to 330 in the listening parts of the TOEIC® is possibly very wide to induce any type of pattern or tendency. Therefore, for further analysis, the score range of 166–330 was sub-divided into two ranges, i.e. low-intermediate (166–249) and upper-intermediate (250–330)

4.4.3 Discussion about the D+LSTG participants whose scores increased and decreased in Week 15

In Study II, the combined teaching method was proven ineffective for EFL intermediate listeners under a certain condition of 60 minutes for 13 weeks. In addition, the scatter plot shows no regular pattern. Figure 4.3 shows that 20 of the 29 participants (69%) in the D+LSTG increased their scores, eight (28%) decreased their scores and only one (3%) showed no change in Week 15.

First, let us observe those participants in the D+LSTG who increased their scores in Week 15. Figure 4.4 presents the percentage of the D+LSTG participants whose scores increased in Week 15. Amongst them, half (i.e. 10 out of 20) were low-intermediate listeners. Judging from these data, the scores of the TOEIC® listening parts in Week 1 are not considered as key factors for measuring whether the combined teaching method is effective for EFL intermediate listeners. It is noticeable that the elements and factors related to improving listening comprehension do not simply rely on the scores of the listening parts of the TOEIC®.

Second, let us focus on the results of those participants who decreased their scores in Week 15. Figure 4.5 shows the percentage of the D+LSTG participants whose scores decreased in Week 15. Amongst them, 88% (seven out of eight) were upper-intermediate listeners, and 12% (one out of eight) were low-intermediate listeners. At this point, it is clear that the majority of the D+LSTG participants who scored more than 250 on the TOEIC® listening parts in Week 1 decreased their scores in Week 15. As per Anderson's (2010) theory, the score of 250 in the listening parts of the TOEIC® is again assumed as a border line of perception, as observed in Study I. However, listening strategies are very complicated and difficult to acquire compared to perception. Furthermore, it is natural to consider that the ability to use appropriate listening strategies based on a task takes more time than perception. Unless phonetic perception is automatically processed, there is almost no capacity to activate adequate listening strategies for listening tasks. Thus, combined training is very demanding for intermediate listeners. Again, these results are consistent with Schneider and Shiffrin's (1977) and Anderson's (2010) claim that there are gradual steps in both human information processing and language acquisition.

Although there were a total of 57 participants in Study II, when focussing on those whose scores increased in the D+LSTG in Week 15, this number was reduced to 20. For further analysis, they were divided into two groups of low- and upper-intermediate listeners, based on their scores in Week 1, but there were only 10 in each group. Similarly, when focussing on those whose scores decreased in the D+LSTG in Week 15, they were a mere eight participants. For further analysis, when they were divided into two groups of low- and upper-intermediate listeners based on their scores in Week 1, there were only one and seven participants, respectively. These numbers are very small to induce any type of assumption. Therefore, as another element for further analysis, the results of the MALQ are discussed in the next section.

4.4.4 Discussion about the MALQ

In this section, the results of the MALQ, which was conducted in both groups in Weeks 1 and 15, are analysed and discussed from a different perspective, i.e. metacognitive awareness before and after the study. As stated earlier, the MALQ is a questionnaire designed by Vandergrift, Goh, Mareschal and Tafaghodtari (2006) regarding metacognitive awareness in EFL/ESL listening with 21 items, six scales (ranging from 1 to 6)[10] and five factors.

The discussion is made as per these five factors, which are mentioned below, by comparing the differences in the CG and D+LSTG before and after the study. Only the items whose difference is 0.5 or more are closely analysed since the difference below 0.5 is considered as nil in this study.

1) Directed Attention; ways of concentrating on certain aspects of a task
2) Mental Translation; translation from English to L1 when listening
3) Person Knowledge;
   confidence or anxiety and self-perception as a listener
4) Planning and Evaluation; preparing to listen and assessing success
5) Problem Solving; guessing as well as monitoring these guesses

First, there are four items that investigate Directed Attention in the MALQ:

---

[10] 1 = Strongly disagree, 2 = Disagree, 3 = Slightly agree, 4 = Partly agree, 5 = Agree and 6 = Strongly agree.

No. 2: I focus harder on the text when I have trouble understanding.
No. 6: When my mind wanders, I recover my concentration right away.
No. 12: I try to get back on track when I lose concentration.
No. 16: When I have difficulty understanding what I hear, I give up and stop listening.

Table 4.14   Differences in the Post-Mean Scores in the CG and D+LSTG about Directed Attention

Directed Attention	2		6		12		16	
	CG	D+LSTG	CG	D+LSTG	CG	D+LSTG	CG	D+LSTG
Wk 1	4.8	4.6	4.2	4.4	4.5	4.6	2.1	2.8
Wk 15	4.7	4.9	3.8	4.6	4.4	4.9	2.7	3.0
D	-0.1	0.3	-0.4	0.2	-0.1	0.3	0.6	0.2

Scale

1	2	3	4	5	6
Strongly disagree	Disagree	Slightly disagree	Partly agree	Agree	Strongly agree

Table 4.14 shows that No. 16 in the CG shows a change with 0.6, which does not represent an improvement in Directed Attention since the post-mean score still remains in the range of 2 (Disagree). Instead, it implies that giving up occurs more easily when facing difficulties understanding and listening to English (Figure 4.6 and Tables 4.7 and 4.14). The post-mean scores of the other three items (i.e. Nos. 2, 6 and 12) show no difference of more than 0.5. Based on these results, it is assumed that Directed Attention does not improve when intermediate listeners receive no special listening training. In addition, they continue having difficulties concentrating and greater tendencies to stop listening when facing difficulties understanding and listening to English.

Now, let us observe the results of the D+LSTG. All the items show an increase of no more than 0.3 (Table 4.14). Again, the results show that the combined training, under the conditions of Study II, has no effect for intermediate listeners to improve Directed Attention in metacognition: They also continue having difficulties concentrating and greater tendencies to stop listening when facing difficulties in understanding and listening to English.

Second, in regard to Mental Translation in metacognition, there are three items in the MALQ:

No. 4:   I translate in my head as I listen.
No. 11:   I translate key words as I listen.
No. 18:   I translate word by word, as I listen.[11]

Table 4.15 Differences in the Post-Mean Scores in the CG and D+LSTG about Mental Translation

Mental Translation	4		11		18	
	CG	D+LSTG	CG	D+LSTG	CG	D+LSTG
Wk 1	4.1	3.8	5.0	4.4	2.6	2.5
Wk 15	3.2	3.6	3.9	4.7	1.9	2.0
D	-0.9	-0.2	-1.1	0.3	-0.7	-0.5

Scale

1	2	3	4	5	6
Strongly disagree	Disagree	Slightly disagree	Partly agree	Agree	Strongly agree

Table 4.15 shows that all three post-mean scores in the CG decreased by more than 0.5. However, this does not represent the deterioration of Mental Translation. Instead, it is an improvement. For example, let us look at No. 11 (i.e. I translate key words as I listen) whose change is the most prominent. Before the study, the mean score of the CG participants was 5.0, which means that they strongly agree to translate key words when listening. However, after the study, it changed to 3.9 (Slightly disagree). In addition,

---

[11] sic

the post-mean scores of Nos. 4 and 18 in the CG changed by more than 0.5. As for No. 4, it changed from 4.1 (Partly agree) to 3.2 (Slightly disagree) for the item: I translate in my head as I listen. As for No. 18, it changed from 2.6 (Disagree) to 1.9 (Strongly disagree) for the item: I translate word by word, as I listen. Based on these results, it is inferred that intermediate listeners can improve Mental Translation in metacognition even when they receive no special listening training.

On the other hand, although No. 18 shows a change of 0.5 from 2.5 to 2.0 in the D+LSTG, the other items do not show any change of more than 0.5 (Table 4.15). These results show that the combined training, under the conditions of Study II, has no effect for intermediate listeners, especially in regard to improving Mental Translation in metacognition.

Third, there are three items regarding Person Knowledge in the MALQ:

No. 3: I find that listening is more difficult than reading, speaking, or writing in English.
No. 8: I feel that listening comprehension in English is a challenge for me.
No.15: I don't[12] feel nervous when I listen to English.

Table 4.16 Differences in the Post-Mean Scores in the CG and D+LSTG about Person Knowledge

Person Knowledge	3		8		15	
	CG	D+LSTG	CG	D+LSTG	CG	D+LSTG
Wk 1	3.2	4.3	4.3	4.2	3.4	3.4
Wk 15	3.5	3.6	4.5	3.9	3.4	3.4
D	0.3	-0.7	0.2	-0.3	0	0

Scale

1	2	3	4	5	6
Strongly disagree	Disagree	Slightly disagree	Partly agree	Agree	Strongly agree

---

[12] sic

According to Table 4.16, none of the post-mean scores of the CG changed more than 0.5. Based on these results, it is assumed that Person Knowledge in metacognition does not seem to improve when intermediate listeners receive no special listening training: They remain nervous and find listening in English challenging without such training.

Now, let us observe the results of the D+LSTG. Although the post-mean score of No. 3 in the D+LSTG shows a change of 0.7 from 4.3 (Partly agree) to 3.6 (Slightly disagree) for the item: I find that listening is more difficult than reading, speaking, or writing in English, No. 15 shows no change, and the post-mean score of No. 8 is no more than 0.5. These results show that the combined training, under the conditions of Study II, has no effect for intermediate listeners to improve Person Knowledge in metacognition: They remain nervous and find listening in English challenging.

Fourth, there are five items regarding Planning/Evaluation in the MALQ:

No. 1: Before I start to listen, I have a plan in my head for how I am going to listen.
No.10: Before listening, I think of similar texts that I may have listened to.
No.14: After listening, I think back to how I listened, and about what I might do differently next time.
No. 20: As I listen, I periodically ask myself if I am satisfied with my level of comprehension.
No. 21: I have a goal in mind as I listen.

Table 4.17 Differences in the Post-Mean Scores in the CG and D+LSTG about Planning/Evaluation

Planning Evaluation	1		10		14		20		21	
	CG	D+LSTG	CG	D+LSTG	CG	D+LSTG	CG	D+LSTG	CG	D+LSTG
Wk 1	4.1	4.0	4.3	4.1	3.8	3.8	3.7	3.6	4.4	4.3
Wk 15	4.5	5.2	4.1	4.9	3.9	4.2	3.7	3.9	4.3	4.9
D	0.4	1.2	-0.2	0.8	0.1	0.4	0	0.3	-0.1	0.6

Scale

1	2	3	4	5	6
Strongly disagree	Disagree	Slightly disagree	Partly agree	Agree	Strongly agree

According to Table 4.17, none of the post-mean scores of the CG changed by more than 0.5. These results show that Planning/Evaluation in metacognition does not seem to improve when intermediate listeners receive no special listening training: They neither plan how they listen nor evaluate how they listened.

Now, let us observe the D+LSTG. Based on several items, the combined training, under the conditions of Study II, seems to be effective for intermediate listeners to improve Planning/Evaluation in metacognition. For instance, No. 1 shows a prominent improvement from 4.0 (Partly agree) to 5.2 (Agree) for the item: Before I start to listen, I have a plan in my head for how I am going to listen. This suggests that the D+LSTG participants agree that they gain the ability to plan how they are going to listen before listening. Although No. 10, with a 0.8 difference, still remains in the range of 4 (Partly agree), it shows a more concrete idea of how they plan and think about similar texts that they may have listened to before listening. In addition, No. 21, with a 0.6 difference, shows an improvement in regard to planning and having a goal in mind when listening. Although Nos. 14 and 20 show no change of more than 0.5, these results show that the combined training, under the conditions of Study II, is effective for intermediate listeners to improve planning but not evaluating/monitoring in metacognition.

Finally, there are six items regarding Problem Solving in the MALQ:

No. 5: I use the words I understand to guess the meaning of the words I don't[13] understand.
No. 7: As I listen, I compare what I understand with what I know about the topic.
No. 9: I use my experience and knowledge to help me understand.
No. 13: As I listen, I quickly adjust my interpretation if I realise that it is not correct.
No. 17: I use the general idea of the text to help me guess the meaning of the words that I don't[14] understand.
No. 19: When I guess the meaning of a word, I think back to everything else that I have heard,[15] to see if my guess makes sense.

Table 4.18   Differences in the Post-Mean Scores in the CG and D+LSTG about Problem Solving

Problem Solving	5		7		9		13		17		19	
	CG	D+LSTG	CG	D+LSTG	CG	D+LSTG	CG	D+LSTG	CG	D+LSTG	CG	D+LSTG
Wk 1	4.8	4.6	4.3	3.7	5.0	4.6	3.6	3.9	4.9	4.5	3.9	3.6
Wk 15	4.7	4.7	4.6	5.0	4.5	5.2	3.8	4.0	4.8	5.2	4.5	4.5
D	-0.1	0.1	0.3	1.3	-0.5	0.6	0.2	0.1	-0.1	0.7	0.6	0.9

Scale

1	2	3	4	5	6
Strongly disagree	Disagree	Slightly disagree	Partly agree	Agree	Strongly agree

---

[13] sic
[14] sic
[15] sic

A closer look at Table 4.18 reveals that the CG shows no change of more than 0.5 apart from No. 19. The 0.5 change in No. 9 does not indicate an improvement since it changes from 5.0 (Agree) to 4.5 (Partly agree) for the item: I use my experience and knowledge to help me understand. The change in No. 19 might mean that intermediate listeners possibly gain the ability to guess the meaning of a word and check if their guess makes sense at a certain degree even without any special listening training. However, the post-mean score indicates that this suggestion is only partly true. Based on these results, it is concluded that intermediate listeners are unable to improve Problem Solving in metacognition without any particular listening training.

Now, let us analyse the results of the D+LSTG. Table 4.18 shows that the most noticeable improvement was in No. 7 since it changed from 3.7 (Slightly disagree) to 5.0 (Agree) for the item: As I listen, I compare what I understand with what I know about the topic. Both post-mean scores of Nos. 9 and 17 show differences of 0.6 and 0.7, respectively. As for No. 19, although the post-mean scores of both the CG and D+LSTG are the same (i.e. 4.5), the change of the D+LSTG is greater than the one of the CG. In addition, Nos. 5 and 13 show no change of more than 0.5. These results show that the combined listening training, under the conditions of Study II, is only somewhat effective for improving Problem Solving in metacognition since Nos. 5 and 13 do not change by more than 0.5.

Thus far, the participants in the CG and D+LSTG have been observed and discussed. Now let us briefly observe the features and changes regarding the metacognitive skills of those in the D+LSTG who increased their scores over 1.0 between the pre- and post-mean scores in the MALQ for further investigation. Figure 4.8, Tables 4.11 and 4.13 show that the top 11 D+LSTG participants made two prominent changes in Planning/Evaluation and three prominent changes in Problem Solving. As for Planning/Evaluation, No. 1 changed from 4.1 (Partly agree) to 5.3 (Agree) for the item: Before I start to listen, I have a plan in my head for how I am going to listen. In addition, No. 14 shows a 1.1 change from 3.4 (Slightly disagree) to 4.5 (Partly agree) for the item: After listening, I think back to how I listened, and about what I might do differently next time. As for the metacognitive skill of Planning/Evaluation, the difference between the D+LSTG participants and the top 11 D+LSTG participants is found in No. 14 or the evaluation of self-comprehension after listening. Thus, the metacognitive skill of thinking back to how one listened and planned to listen differently for the next time could be a vital skill for improving one's listening comprehension.

Prominent changes were also found in Problem Solving. No. 7, which changed from 3.7 (Slightly disagree) to 5.4 (Agree) for the item: As I listen, I compare what I understand with what I know about the topic. No. 9 also changed from 4.4 (Partly agree) to 5.4 (Agree) for the item: I use my experience and knowledge to help me understand. Furthermore, No. 17 changed from 4.2 (Partly agree) to 5.5 (Agree) for the item: I use the general idea of the text to help me guess the meaning of the words that I don't[16] understand. Although the D+LSTG parti cipants also showed an improvement in Nos. 7, 9 and 17 (Table 4.13), the top 11 participants in this group made prominent changes of more than 1.0 in Nos. 9 and 17. Furthermore, these top 11 D+LSTG participants showed more improvement (1.7) than the D+LSTG participants (1.3) in No. 7 (Tables 4.8 and 4.11). Therefore, in addition to the metacognitive skill of Planning/Evaluation, Problem Solving could be another vital skill for improving listening comprehension in EFL. Based on these results, an improvement of Planning/Evaluation and Problem Solving in metacognitive skills can be the key to become a successful listener.

4.5 Summary

S-1 For intermediate listeners, the combined training of dictation training and listening strategy training is not effective.

---

[16] sic

S-2 For intermediate listeners, combined listening training is not effective for improving metacognitive skills in EFL listening such as Directed Attention, Mental Translation and Person knowledge.

S-3 An improvement in Planning/Evaluation and Problem Solving in metacognitive skills are vital for becoming advanced listeners in EFL listening

A total of 57 Japanese learners of English participated in Study II. Only those who scored between 166 and 330 in the listening part of the TOEIC® in Week 1 were selected after which they were divided into two groups, i.e. the CG (28) and the D+LSTG (29). During Weeks 2 and 14, the CG participants had no training other than their usual 90-minute class each week. The D+LSTG participants received combined training of both dictation training and listening strategy training for approximately 30 minutes each in their usual 90-minute class. In Week 15, all the participants took the same listening parts of the TOEIC® as in Week 1.

Although 69% of the D+LSTG participants increased their scores in Week 15, both the CG and D+LSTG showed almost an identical change. The results reveal that the combined training has no significant effect on intermediate listeners. Although the effect was significant for intermediate listeners when these two types of training were separately provided for both groups in Study I, this was not the case when the training was combined. This finding indicates that the amount of information provided through combined training can be excessive to put into practice for intermediate listeners. In addition, significance was not observed in the increases of the D+LSTG with a two-way ANOVA. This result supports both theories of Schneider and Shiffrin (1977) and Anderson (2010) as well as Hypothesis 1.

Finally, it was also found that the combined listening training is hardly effective for improving metacognitive skills. However, based on the features in the MALQ of the top 11 participants who increased their scores in the listening parts of the TOEIC® in Week 15, it can be concluded that an improvement of Planning/Evaluation and Problem Solving is critical to become an advanced EFL listener.

Chapter 5: Study III—Dictation Training and Listening Strategy Training with the MALQ

5.1 Hypotheses

Study III investigates two aspects in particular: The reliability of the results obtained in Study I and the individual influence of dictation training and listening strategy training on metacognitive awareness in EFL listening. As stated in Chapter 3, both dictation training and listening strategy training were significantly effective for Japanese EFL intermediate listeners in Study I. In addition, dictation training was significantly effective, especially for lower-intermediate listeners who scored less than 250 in the listening parts of the TOEIC® in Week 1. These results of Study I are consistent with the theories of Schneider and Shiffrin (1977) and Anderson (2010) in which there are gradual steps in both human information processing and language comprehension. However, there were only 10 participants in the CG, and the MALQ was not conducted in Study I.

As for the synergetic influence of dictation training and listening strategy training on metacognitive awareness in EFL listening, it was observed that, in Study II, the combined listening training does not improve some metacognitive skills in EFL listening such as Directed Attention, Mental Translation and Person Knowledge. Nonetheless, since these two types of training were combined and provided to only one group, the influence of each training on metacognitive skills in EFL listening has not been investigated. Based on the theory of Schneider and Shiffrin (1977), dictation in listening is categorised as controlled processing (bottom-up processing) since it involves phonemic decoding, which requires conscious attention to phonemes, the smallest segments of sound (Ladefoged, 1982). In contrast, from a listening strategy perspective, the identification of individual words is mainly regarded as automatic processing (top-down processing), because it can only be possible after phonemic decoding occurs automatically without active control and conscious attention. The less automatic an activity becomes, the more time and cognitive energy it requires. Accordingly, if dictation training was provided more frequently (i.e. more than once a week, more than 30 minutes and more than 13 weeks), then their phonemic decoding would become much more automatic. However, without being instructed on what metacognitive skills are and their effectiveness in EFL listening, it would be extremely unusual for the participants to begin spontaneously employing listening strategies in EFL, especially since Japanese learners of English are rarely instructed in listening strategies during junior and senior high school. In this regard, the influence of listening strategy training on metacognition in EFL listening is assumed to be greater than that of dictation training especially for upper-intermediate listeners. Therefore, the following hypotheses are posited in Study III:

H-1   For intermediate listeners, both dictation training and listening strategy training are effective with significance.

H-2   For low-intermediate listeners, dictation training is more effective.

H-3   For upper-intermediate listeners, listening strategy training is more effective.

H-4   Intermediate listeners with listening strategy training show a greater change in their metacognitive skills.

5.2 Method
5.2.1 Participants

The participants in Study III consisted of 94 first-year students (in the Faculty of Economics) at a Japanese private university who were administered the listening parts of the TOEIC® in September 2013. Only those who scored between 166 and 330 were selected as the participants in Study III, as in Studies I and II. None of the participants' major subject was English, and the classes were part of the regular English curriculum. The participants were divided into three groups, i.e. 23 in the CG, which was part of the EFL listening class; 34 in the DTG, with half of them belonging to the general English class and the other half belonging to the EFL reading class and 37 in the LSTG, with half of them belonging to the EFL reading class and the other half belonging to the EFL listening class. All the lessons were presented in English as per the policy of the faculty. Initially there were more participants, but only those who attended all 15 classes between September 2013 and January 2014 were selected for Study III. Table 5.1 summarises the means, SDs and relative values of these three groups in Week 1.

Table 5.1 Numbers, Means and SDs of the CG, DTG and LSTG in Week 1 of Study III

Group	N	Mean	SD
CG	23	202.83	26.36
DTG	34	241.91	39.16
LSTG	37	242.84	32.22

A one-way ANOVA was conducted for their scores of the listening parts of the TOEIC®, and the results show that there was significance amongst these three groups ($F(2, 91) = 11.99, p < 0.001$). Through Ryan's method, significance amongst these three groups was also observed (Table 5.2). However, there was no significance between the DTG and LSTG. Although significance was observed between the CG and DTG and the CG and LSTG, respectively, only those who scored between 166 and 330 on the listening parts of the TOEIC® in Week 1 were selected for Study III.

Table 5.2   Results of Ryan's Method on the Three Groups before Study III

	CG	DTG	LSTG
mean :	202.83	241.91	242.84
n :	23	34	37

pair	r	nominal level	t	p	sig.
LSTG–CG	3	0.02	4.47	0.00	s.
LSTG–DTG	2	0.03	0.12	0.91	n.s.
DTG –CG	2	0.03	4.30	0.00	s.

$MSe = 1134.82$, $df = 91$, $significance\ level = 0.05$

5.2.2 Materials

Both the MALQ (used in Study II) and the same listening parts of the TOEIC® (conducted in Studies I and II) were administered for all three groups before and after Study III. In addition, for the DTG and LSTG, the same teaching materials in Study I were used.

5.2.3 Procedure

For Study III, the same procedure used in Study I was conducted. In Week 1 of the second term in 2013, 94 participants were selected based on their TOEIC® listening scores. From Weeks 2 to 14, both the DTG and LSTG participants were trained for 30 minutes[17] (with instructions in Japanese) as part of the 90-minute regular class. The procedure of the dictation training was as follows.

In Step 1, the DTG participants were first informed about the purpose and subject of the training, after which they listened to the relevant parts of the CD (attached to the textbook) only once. Whilst listening, they dictated some words/phrases/short sentences on the provided handouts, which the present author had created based on the textbook's exercise page. Then, the

---

[17] Due to the inflexible class syllabus, only 30 minutes were allowed for the study.

answers were provided.

In Step 2, the participants viewed the answers whilst listening to the CD for a second time to combine the words/phrases/short sentences that they were unable to dictate *with* the acoustic information.

In Step 3, the participants listened to the CD a third time *without* looking at the answers to comprehend the words/phrases or short sentences that they were unable to dictate purely through the acoustic information.

The LSTG participants were first instructed on the logical aspects of the relevant listening strategies for that lesson. Then, they performed listening tasks that involved applying the instructed listening strategies, after which they were provided with the answers and pertinent feedback.

In Week 15, the participants answered the listening parts of the TOEIC®. Although this test was identical to that of Week 1, the participants were not provided with the answers of the initial test and were not informed that the same test would be used in Week 15. This guaranteed the test's validity and allowed us to compare the scores obtained in Weeks 1 and 15.

5.3 Results

The effectiveness of the two types of teaching methods (i.e. dictation training and listening strategy training) for intermediate listeners in EFL listening were investigated. The data concerning the differences for the three groups (i.e. the CG, DTG and LSTG) between Weeks 1 and 15 on the listening parts of the TOEIC® are presented, followed by an analysis and a discussion of the data. After the discussion of the effectiveness regarding these two types of teaching methods, more detailed observations that focus on both low- and upper-intermediate listeners are made.

First, a two-way ANOVA was conducted with two factors, i.e. 'teaching methods' (for the CG, DTG and LSTG) and 'before and after Study III'. Figure 5.1 presents the relative values of the CG, DTG and LSTG scores by comparing Weeks 1 and 15. Table 5.3 summarises the means, SDs and relative values of these three groups in Weeks 1 and 15.

A quick look at Figure 5.1 shows sharp increases in both the DTG and LSTG.

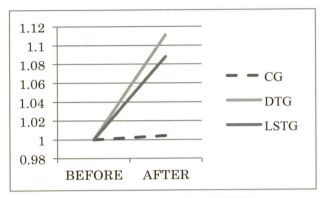

Figure 5.1 Relative values of the CG, DTG and LSTG scores by comparing Weeks 1 and 15 of Study III

Table 5.3 Numbers, Means, SDs, Relative Values and Means of Differences of the CG, DTG and LSTG in Weeks 1 and 15 of Study III

	Week 1			Week 15			
	N	Mean	SD	Mean	SD	Relative Value	Mean of difference
CG	23	202.83	26.36	203.70	31.20	1.00	0.87
DTG	34	241.91	39.16	268.82	47.26	1.11	26.91
LSTG	37	242.84	32.22	264.19	30.88	1.09	21.35

Table 5.4 presents the results of the two-way ANOVA and Ryan's method, which were conducted in accordance with the null hypothesis (Table 5.5). The findings show that dictation training is more effective than listening strategy training and that both the training methods are significantly effective for intermediate listeners.

Table 5.4 Results of the Two-way ANOVA in Study III

Source	SS	df	MS	F	p
A: Teaching Methods	104964.7	2	52482.36	25.5	0.00 ****
Error[S(A)]	187325.7	91	2058.52		
B: Before & After	12080.12	1	12080.12	24.22	0.00 ****
AB	5647.77	2	2823.89	5.66	0.01 ***
Error[BS(A)]	45382.89	91	498.71		

$+p < .10$, $*p < .05$, $**p < .01$, $***p < .005$, $****p < .001$

Table 5.5 Results of Ryan's Method in Study III

	CG	DTG	LSTG
mean :	203.261	255.368	253.514
n :	46	68	74

pair	r	nominal level	t	p	sig.
DTG–CG	3	0.02	6.02	0.00	s.
DTG–LSTG	2	0.03	0.24	0.81	n.s.
LSTG–CG	2	0.03	5.90	0.00	s.

$MSe = 2058.52$, $df = 91$, significance level = 0.05

The effect size of Factor A (teaching methods), Factor B (before and after the study) and the interaction between Factors A and B are large, small and small, respectively (Table 5.6).

Table 5.6 Effect Sizes in Study III

$\eta 2$ in Factor A (Teaching Methods)	2.31
$\eta 2$ in Factor B (Before and After)	0.27
$\eta 2$ in Interaction of Factors A and B	0.13

Effect Size (r): small = 0.10, medium = 0.30, large = 0.50

A quick look at Figure 5.2 shows that there are no regular patterns.

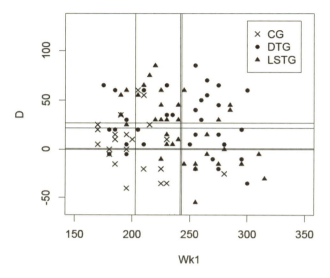

Figure 5.2 **Scatter plot of Study III**

In the DTG, there were 34 participants, i.e. 27 participants (79%) increased their scores and seven participants (21%) decreased their scores in Week 15 (Figure 5.3).

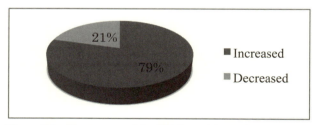

Figure 5.3 **Percentage of the DTG participants' score change in Week 15 of Study III**

Study III - Dictation Training and Listening Strategy Training with the MALQ

In the DTG, 27 of the 34 participants increased their scores in Week 15, and 12 of these 27 participants (44%) scored less than 250, whereas 15 participants (56%) scored 250 or more in Week 1 (Figure 5.4).

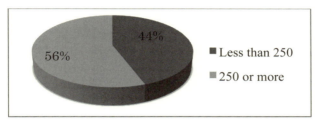

Figure 5.4   Score proportion in Week 1 of the DTG participants whose scores increased in Week 15 of Study III

Another two-way ANOVA was conducted for further investigation on the effect of dictation training between low- and upper-intermediate listeners based on their scores of the listening parts of the TOEIC® in Week 1. There were 14 upper- and 20 low- intermediate listeners in the DTG. The results show that there was no significance in the interaction between these two groups (Table 5.7).

Table 5.7   Results of the Two-way ANOVA on the Effect of Dictation Training between Low- and Upper-Intermediate Listeners in Study III

Source	SS	df	MS	F	p
A: More & Less than 250[S(A)]	76200.01	1	76200.01	74.11	0.00 ****
Error[S(A)]	32903.30	32	1028.23		
B: Before & After	12246.48	1	12246.48	25.90	0.00 **
AB	67.06	1	67.07	0.14	0.71
Error[BS(A)]	15133.30	32	472.92		

$+ p<.10, * p<.05, ** p<.01, *** p<.005, **** p<.001$

On the contrary, in the LSTG, there were 37 participants of which 25 (67%) increased their scores, 11 participants (30%) decreased their scores and one participant (3%) showed no change in Week 15 (Figure 5.5).

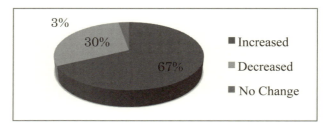

Figure 5.5 Percentage of the LSTG participants' score change in Week 15 of Study III

In the LSTG, 25 of the 37 participants increased their scores in Week 15, as mentioned earlier (Figure 5.5), and 21 of these 25 participants (84%) were low-intermediate listeners, whilst four participants (16%) were upper-intermediate listeners (Figure 5.6).

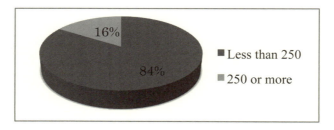

Figure 5.6 Score proportion in Week 1 of the LSTG participants whose scores increased in Week 15 of Study III

Another two-way ANOVA was conducted for further investigation on the effect of listening strategy training between low- and upper-intermediate listeners based on their scores on the listening parts of the TOEIC® in Week 1. There were 14 upper- and 23 low-intermediate listeners in the LSTG. The results show that there was significance in the interaction between the two groups at the 0.1% level (Table 5.8).

Table 5.8　Results of the Two-way ANOVA on the Effect of Listening Strategy Training between Low- and Upper-Intermediate Listeners in Study III

Source	SS	df	MS	F	p
A: More & Less than 250[S(A)]	20109.62	1	20109.62	22.10	0.00****
Error[S(A)]	31851.86	35	910.05		
B: Before & After	4724.36	1	4724.36	12.97	0.00****
AB	6994.63	1	6994.63	19.21	0.00 ****
Error[BS(A)]	12746.58	35	364.19		

$+p < .10$, $*p < .05$, $**p < .01$, $***p < .005$, $****p < .001$

Therefore, means for the interaction between 'low/upper intermediate listeners' and 'before/after the study' as well as the simple main effect of the interaction between Factors A and B were calculated. The results show that there was significance on the effect of listening strategy training for upper-intermediate listeners at the 0.1% level (Tables 5.9 and 5.10).

Table 5.9　Means of the Interaction between Factors A (Low- and Upper-Intermediate Listeners) and B (before/after the Study) in the LSTG of Study III

Factor A=1 (Upper-Intermediate Listeners)			Factor A=2 (Low-Intermediate Listeners)		
B->	1	2	B->	1	2
mean	276.43	272.86	mean	222.39	258.91
n	14	14	n	23	23

Table 5.10 Simple Main Effect Test of Listening Strategy Training between Low- and Upper-Intermediate Listeners in Study III

Effect	SS	df	MS	F	p
A(b1)	25412.12	1	25412.12	39.89	0.00 ****
A(b2)	1692.14	1	1692.14	2.66	0.11
Error		70	637.12		
B(a1)	11607.99	1	11607.99	31.87	0.00 ****
B(a2)	111.00	1	111.00	0.31	0.58
Error		35	364.19		

$+p < .10, *p < .05, **p < .01, ***p < .005, ****p < .001$

Although the majority of the participants in both the DTG (79%) and LSTG (67%) improved their scores in Week 15 (Figures 5.3 and 5.5), it was also observed that many participants in both groups decreased their scores in Week 15. For example, in the DTG, seven participants decreased their scores in Week 15, and five out of these seven participants (71%) were upper-intermediate listeners (Figure 5.7 below).

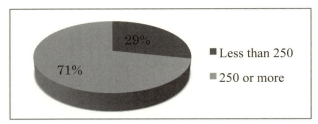

Figure 5.7 Score proportion in Week 1 of the DTG participants whose scores decreased in Week 15 of Study III

On the other hand, in the LSTG, 11 participants decreased their scores in Week 15, and nine of these 11 participants (82%) were upper-intermediate listeners, whereas two of these 11 participants (18%) were low-intermediate listeners (Figure 5.8).

Study III - Dictation Training and Listening Strategy Training with the MALQ

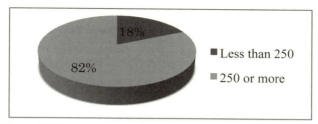

Figure 5.8 Score proportion in Week 1 of the LSTG participants whose scores decreased in Week 15 of Study III

A quick look at Figure 5.9 shows the pre- and post-mean scores of the CG on the MALQ in Study III.

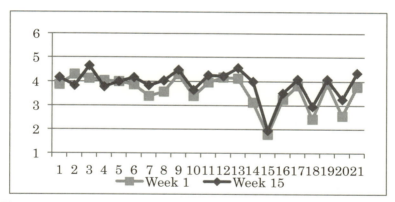

Figure 5.9 Pre- and post-mean scores of the CG on the MALQ in Study III

According to Table 5.11, Nos. 5 and 12 showed no change, the mean scores of Nos. 2 and 4 decreased and the others increased after the study.

Table 5.11 Pre- and Post-Mean Scores of the CG on the MALQ in Study III

CG	1	2	3	4	5	6	7	8	9	10	11	12	13	14	15	16	17	18	19	20	21
Wk 1	3.9	4.3	4.1	4	4	3.9	3.4	3.6	4.3	3.4	4	4.2	4.1	3.1	1.8	3.3	3.8	2.4	3.9	2.6	3.8
Wk 15	4.2	3.8	4.7	3.8	4	4.2	3.8	4	4.5	3.7	4.3	4.2	4.6	4	2	3.5	4.1	3	4.1	3.3	4.3
D	0.3	-0.5	0.6	-0.2	0	0.3	0.4	0.4	0.2	0.3	0.3	0	0.5	0.9	0.2	0.2	0.3	0.6	0.2	0.7	0.5

Figure 5.10 presents the pre- and post-mean scores of the DTG on the MALQ in Study III.

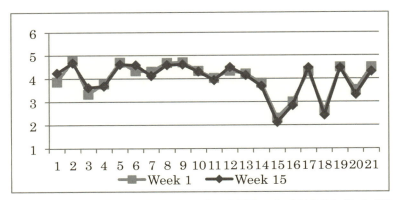

Figure 5.10 Pre- and post-mean scores of the DTG on the MALQ in Study III

Table 5.12 displays that Nos. 10, 13 and 19 showed no change, the mean scores of Nos. 1, 3, 6, 12 and 17 increased and the others decreased after the study.

Table 5.12 Pre- and Post-Mean Scores of the DTG on the MALQ in Study III

DTG	1	2	3	4	5	6	7	8	9	10	11	12	13	14	15	16	17	18	19	20	21
Wk 1	3.9	4.8	3.3	3.8	4.7	4.3	4.3	4.7	4.7	4.3	4	4.3	4.2	3.8	2.3	3	4.3	2.6	4.5	3.5	4.5
Wk 15	4.3	4.7	3.6	3.7	4.6	4.6	4.1	4.6	4.6	4.3	3.9	4.5	4.2	3.7	2.1	2.8	4.5	2.4	4.5	3.3	4.3
D	0.4	-0.1	0.3	-0.1	-0.1	0.3	-0.2	-0.1	-0.1	0	-0.1	0.2	0	-0.1	-0.2	-0.2	0.2	-0.2	0	-0.2	-0.2

Figure 5.11 presents the pre- and post-mean scores of the LSTG on the MALQ in Study III.

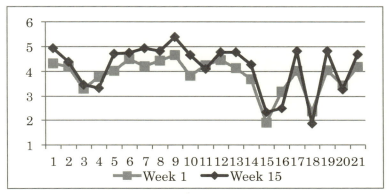

Figure 5.11   Pre- and post-mean scores of the LSTG on the MALQ in Study III

Table 5.13 shows that the mean scores of Nos. 4, 11, 16, 18 and 20 decreased, whereas the others increased after the study.

Table 5.13   Pre- and Post-Mean Scores of the LSTG on the MALQ in Study III

LSTG	1	2	3	4	5	6	7	8	9	10	11	12	13	14	15	16	17	18	19	20	21
Wk 1	4.3	4.2	3.3	3.8	4	4.5	4.2	4.4	4.7	3.8	4.3	4.5	4.1	3.7	1.9	3.2	4	2.4	4.1	3.4	4.2
Wk 15	4.9	4.4	3.5	3.3	4.7	4.8	4.9	4.8	5.4	4.7	4.1	4.8	4.8	4.3	2.3	2.5	4.8	1.9	4.8	3.3	4.7
D	0.6	0.2	0.2	-0.5	0.7	0.3	0.7	0.4	0.7	0.9	-0.2	0.3	0.7	0.6	0.4	-0.7	0.8	-0.5	0.8	-0.1	0.5

For further analysis on metacognitive awareness before and after the study, the DTG participants were divided into two categories, i.e. the top 10 participants who improved their scores and the bottom seven participants who lowered their scores in Week 15. Amongst the top 10 participants, two of the original 10 participants were excluded since there was no MALQ data for these individuals. Therefore, the top 11th and 12th participants were included in the top 10 list. In addition, only seven participants decreased their scores in the DTG in Week 15. For more details on these participants, see Tables 5.14 and 5.15.

Table 5.14   Scores of the Top 10 DTG Participants whose Scores Increased in Week 15 of Study III

Participants	Week 1	Week 15	Differences	Rank
1	255	340	85	1
2	265	335	70	2
3	275	340	65	3
4	230	295	65	3
5	175	240	65	3
6	185	245	60	6
7	265	320	55	7
8	260	310	50	8
9	275	320	45	9
10	255	295	40	10

Table 5.15   Scores of the Bottom Seven DTG Participants whose Scores Decreased in Week 15 of Study III

Participants	Week 1	Week 15	Differences	Rank
1	300	265	-35	1
2	275	255	-20	2
3	255	235	-20	2
4	295	285	-10	4
5	270	260	-10	4
6	195	190	-5	7
7	180	175	-5	7

Figure 5.12 presents the pre- and post-mean scores of the top 10 DTG participants on the MALQ in Study III.

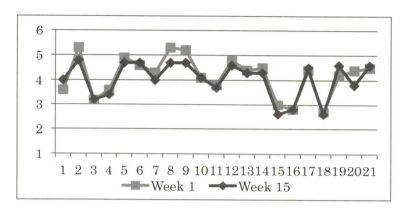

Figure 5.12 Pre- and post-mean scores of the top 10 DTG participants on the MALQ in Study III

Table 5.16 shows a summary of the changes regarding the metacognitive awareness of the top 10 DTG participants before and after the study. According to the table, Nos. 3, 10 and 16 showed no change, the mean scores of Nos. 1, 6, 17, 19 and 21 increased and the others decreased after the study.

Table 5.16 Pre- and Post-Mean Scores of the Top 10 DTG Participants whose Scores Increased on the MALQ in Study III

DTG Top 10	1	2	3	4	5	6	7	8	9	10	11	12	13	14	15	16	17	18	19	20	21
Wk 1	3.6	5.3	3.2	3.6	4.9	4.6	4.3	5.3	5.2	4.1	3.8	4.8	4.4	4.5	3	2.8	4.4	2.7	4.2	4.4	4.5
Wk 15	4	4.8	3.2	3.4	4.7	4.7	4	4.7	4.7	4.1	3.7	4.6	4.3	4.3	2.6	2.8	4.5	2.6	4.6	3.8	4.6
D	0.4	-0.5	0	-0.2	-0.2	0.1	-0.3	-0.6	-0.5	0	-0.1	-0.2	-0.1	-0.2	-0.4	0	0.1	-0.1	0.4	-0.6	0.1

Next, Figure 5.13 presents the pre- and post-mean scores of the bottom seven DTG participants on the MALQ in the in Study III.

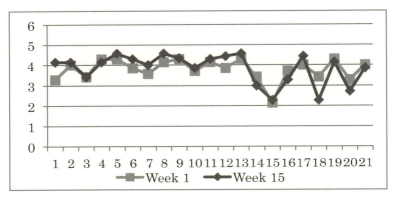

Figure 5.13 Pre- and post-mean scores of the bottom seven DTG participants on the MALQ in Study III

Table 5.17 shows a summary of the changes regarding the metacognitive awareness of the bottom seven DTG participants before and after the study. According to the table, Nos. 3 and 9 showed no change, the mean scores of Nos. 4, 14, 16, 18, 19, 20 and 21 decreased and the others increased after the study.

Table 5.17 Pre- and Post-Mean Scores of the Bottom Seven DTG Participants whose Scores Decreased on the MALQ in Study III

DTG Bottom 7	1	2	3	4	5	6	7	8	9	10	11	12	13	14	15	16	17	18	19	20	21
Wk 1	3.3	4	3.4	4.3	4.3	3.9	3.6	4.1	4.3	3.7	4.1	3.9	4.3	3.4	2.1	3.7	4	3.4	4.3	3.3	4
Wk 15	4.1	4.1	3.4	4.1	4.6	4.3	4	4.6	4.3	3.9	4.3	4.4	4.6	3	2.3	3.3	4.4	2.3	4.1	2.7	3.9
D	0.8	0.1	0	-0.2	0.3	0.4	0.4	0.5	0	0.2	0.2	0.5	0.3	-0.4	0.2	-0.4	0.4	-1.1	-0.2	-0.6	-0.1

Regarding the LSTG, for further analysis on metacognitive awareness before and after the study, the participants were divided into two categories, i.e. the top 12 participants who improved their scores and the bottom 10 participants who lowered the scores in Week 15. Amongst the bottom 10 participants, one participant was excluded since there was no MALQ data for this individual. Therefore, the bottom 11th participant was included in the bottom 10 list. For more details on these participants, see Tables 5.18 and 5.19.

Table 5.18 Scores of the Top 12 LSTG Participants whose Scores Increased in Week 15 of Study III

Participants	Week 1	Week 15	Differences	Rank
1	220	305	85	1
2	215	290	75	2
3	210	275	65	3
4	245	305	60	4
5	225	285	60	4
6	195	255	60	4
7	205	260	55	7
8	190	245	55	7
9	285	330	45	9
10	240	285	45	9
11	240	285	45	9
12	225	270	45	9

Table 5.19 Scores of the Bottom 10 LSTG Participants whose Scores Decreased in Week 15 of Study III

Participants	Week 1	Week 15	Differences	Rank
1	255	200	-55	1
2	315	285	-30	2
3	255	235	-20	3
4	255	235	-20	3
5	275	260	-15	5
6	255	240	-15	5
7	245	230	-15	5
8	225	215	-10	8
9	310	305	-5	9
10	265	260	-5	9

Figure 5.14 presents the pre- and post-mean scores of the top 12 LSTG participants on the MALQ in Study III.

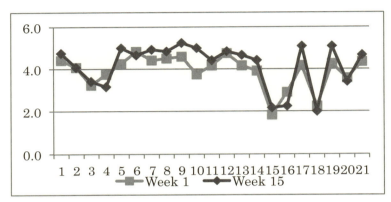

Figure 5.14 Pre- and post-mean scores of the top 12 LSTG participants whose scores increased on the MALQ in Study III

Table 5.20 shows a summary of the changes regarding the metacognitive awareness of the top 12 LSTG participants before and after the study. According to the table, No. 2 showed no change, the mean scores of Nos. 4, 6, 16, 18 and 20 decreased and the others increased after the study.

Table 5.20 Pre- and Post-Mean Scores of the Top 12 LSTG Participants whose Scores Increased on the MALQ in Study III

LSTG Top 12	1	2	3	4	5	6	7	8	9	10	11	12	13	14	15	16	17	18	19	20	21
Wk 1	4.4	4.1	3.3	3.8	4.3	4.8	4.4	4.5	4.6	3.8	4.2	4.8	4.2	3.9	1.8	2.9	4.2	2.3	4.3	3.6	4.3
Wk 15	4.8	4.1	3.4	3.2	5	4.7	4.9	4.8	5.3	5	4.4	4.8	4.7	4.4	2.2	2.3	5.1	2	5.1	3.4	4.7
D	0.4	0	0.1	-0.6	0.7	-0.1	0.5	0.3	0.7	1.2	0.2	0	0.5	0.5	0.4	-0.6	0.9	-0.3	0.8	-0.2	0.4

Study III - Dictation Training and Listening Strategy Training with the MALQ

Next, Figure 5.15 presents the pre- and post-mean scores of the bottom 10 LSTG participants on the MALQ in the in Study III.

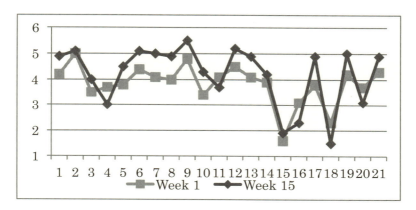

Figure 5.15 Pre- and post-mean scores of the bottom 10 LSTG participants whose scores decreased on the MALQ in Study III

Table 5.21 shows a summary of the changes regarding the metacognitive awareness of the bottom 10 LSTG participants before and after the study. According to the table, the mean scores of Nos. 4, 11, 16, 18 and 20 decreased and the others increased after the study.

Table 5.21 Pre- and Post-Mean Scores of the Bottom 10 LSTG Participants whose Scores Decreased on the MALQ in Study III

LSTG Bottom 10	1	2	3	4	5	6	7	8	9	10	11	12	13	14	15	16	17	18	19	20	21
Wk 1	4.2	5	3.5	3.7	3.8	4.4	4.1	4	4.8	3.4	4.1	4.5	4.1	3.9	1.6	3.1	3.8	2.3	4.2	3.7	4.3
Wk 15	4.9	5.1	4	3	4.5	5.1	5	4.9	5.5	4.3	3.7	5.2	4.9	4.2	1.9	2.3	4.9	1.5	5	3.1	4.9
D	0.7	0.1	0.5	-0.7	0.7	0.7	0.9	0.9	0.7	0.9	-0.4	0.7	0.8	0.3	0.3	-0.8	1.1	-0.8	0.8	-0.6	0.6

Table 5.22 shows a summary of the changes regarding metacognitive awareness in the CG, DTG and LSTG. Both the DTG and LSTG are further divided into two groups.

Table 5.22 Summary of the MALQ before and after Study III

Item No.	Categories	CG	DTG	Top 10	Bottom 7	LSTG	Top 12	Bottom 10
1	Planning/evaluation	△	△	△	△	△	△	△
2	Directed attention	↓	↓	↓	△	△	−	△
3	Person knowledge	△	△	−	−	△	△	△
4	Mental translation	↓	↓	↓	↓	↓	↓	↓
5	Problem-solving	−	↓	↓	△	△	△	△
6	Directed attention	△	△	△	△	△	↓	△
7	Problem-solving	△	↓	↓	△	△	△	△
8	Person knowledge	△	↓	↓	△	△	△	△
9	Problem-solving	△	↓	↓	−	△	△	△
10	Planning/evaluation	△	−	−	△	△	○	△
11	Mental translation	△	↓	↓	△	↓	△	↓
12	Directed attention	−	△	↓	△	△	△	△
13	Problem-solving	△	−	↓	△	△	△	△
14	Planning/evaluation	△	↓	↓	↓	△	△	△
15	Person knowledge	△	↓	↓	△	△	△	△
16	Directed attention	△	↓	−	↓	↓	↓	↓
17	Problem-solving	△	△	△	△	△	△	○
18	Mental translation	△	↓	↓	↓↓	↓	↓	↓
19	Problem-solving	△	−	△	↓	△	△	△
20	Planning/evaluation	△	↓	↓	↓	↓	↓	↓
21	Planning/evaluation	△	↓	△	↓	△	△	△

○: Increased more than 1.0

△: Increased less than 1.0

−: No change

↓: Decreased less than 1.0

↓↓: Decreased over 1.0

5.4 Discussion

The results, as illustrated in the figures and tables, are discussed in the following order:

1. Pre- and post-data for the CG, DTG and LSTG
2. Two-way ANOVA, multiple comparison, effect size and scatter plot
3. The DTG and LSTG participants whose scores increased in Week 15
4. The DTG and LSTG participants whose scores decreased in Week 15
5. The MALQ

5.4.1 Discussion about the pre- and post-data for the CG, DTG and LSTG

The participants of the CG only received regular lessons for 13 weeks, and there was almost no improvement in their listening comprehension (Figure 5.1). This result is different from that of Study I in which there was some improvement even in the CG (Figure 3.1 in Chapter 3). These two results confirm that listening comprehension can possibly improve even without any particular training, but the level of improvement is not prominent and the process is significantly time consuming. On the contrary, both the DTG and LSTG showed sharp increases, thus demonstrating that both dictation training and listening strategy training are effective for intermediate listeners under certain conditions (in this case, 30 minutes a week for 13 weeks). This result is similar to that of Study I.

As shown in Table 5.3, in Week 1, the mean scores of the CG, DTG and LSTG were 202.83, 241.91 and 242.84, respectively, whereas in Week 15, the mean scores were 203.70, 268.82 and 264.19, respectively. To compare these data as the relative values, the mean scores of each group in Week 1 were treated as 1.00 and compared with those in Week 15. The relative values of the CG, DTG and LSTG were 1.00, 1.11 and 1.09, respectively. The LSTG had the highest mean score in Week 1, but the most prominent improvement was observed in the DTG. The same result was obtained in Study I. Both results indicate that dictation training is more suitable than listening strategy training for intermediate learners. Thus far, the major results of Studies I and III match and correspond with the theories of Schneider and Shiffrin (1977) and Anderson (2010). As referred in Chapter 3, Nation and Newton (2009) also support the importance of bottom-up processes such as dictation training in listening; 'learners need to be proficient with these bottom-up processes and…learners can benefit from being taught how to listen' (p. 41). The following section analyses the data from a different perspective.

5.4.2 Discussion about the two-way ANOVA, multiple comparison, effect size and scatter plot

A two-way ANOVA was conducted on two factors, i.e. 'teaching methods' and 'before/after the study'. In addition, significance was observed in both the factors and in the interaction between these two factors, as shown in Table 5.4. In addition, there was significance in both 'teaching methods' and 'before and after the study' at the 0.1% level. In addition, there was significance in the interaction between these two factors at the 0.5% level. Thus, Ryan's method was utilised for further analysis. The results show significance between the CG and DTG as well as between the CG and LSTG, though no significance was found between the DTG and LSTG (Table 5.5). Again, the same results were obtained in Study I. Note that listening strategy training is *also* significantly effective after dictation training for intermediate listeners. The results of both Studies I and III support the research results of Graham et al. (2008), Vogley (1995), Vandergrift (1997; 1998) and Baleghizadeh and Rahimi (2011), who all claim that strategy development seems to be related to proficiency issues.

In Study III, the effect size of the teaching methods was 2.31, which suggests that both dictation training and listening strategy training are significantly effective (Table 5.6). Again, this result is the same as in Study I. Many researchers, such as Oller (1971), support the effect of dictation training specifically for less-proficient listeners. Yonezaki (2014) also emphasises the effectiveness of dictation since most Japanese learners of English have problems in perception (which is vital for bottom-up processing) and due to such issues, they are unable to activate syntactic knowledge and background knowledge (p. 2). Although Buck (2001, p. 75) indicates that there are various ways of scoring dictation and Hughes (1989) suggests that scoring for low-ability test takers can be difficult since it is not always clear which part of the text their responses refer to, dictation training is effective to solve problems at the perception level.

For the reason that listening strategy training is effective for intermediate learners, it can be considered that they are capable of employing listening strategies to some extent even though their perception level has not been fully automatised. Thus, they could maintain a certain capacity for instructed listening strategies. This assumption is supported by both the effect size of Factor B ('before and after the study'), which is 0.27 (between small and medium) and the effect size of the interaction between Factors A and B, which is 0.13 (between small and medium). These results indicate that there is effectiveness in 'teaching methods', 'before and after the study' and the interaction between these two factors.

Next, a closer examination of the scatter plot reveals that there is no regular pattern and that even some CG participants increased their scores, whereas participants in the DTG and LSTG decreased their scores in Week 15 (Figure 5.2). Based on these findings, it is assumed that the score range between 166 and 330 in the listening parts of the TOEIC® is possibly very wide to induce any type of pattern or tendency. Thus, for further analysis, the score range of 166–330 was sub-divided into two ranges, i.e. 166–249 as low-intermediate and 250–330 as upper-intermediate.

5.4.3 Discussion about the DTG and LSTG participants whose scores increased in Week 15

First, let us observe those participants in the DTG who increased their score in Week 15. Figure 5.3 shows that 27 of the 34 participants (79%) in the DTG increased their scores in Week 15, and 12 of the 27 participants (44%) were low-intermediate listeners (Figure 5.4). The majority of those participants in the DTG who increased their scores in Week 15 were upper-intermediate listeners in Study III. Then, for a further analysis, a two-way ANOVA was conducted on two factors, i.e. 'more/less than 250 in Week 1' and 'before/after the study'. The results show that there was no significance in the interaction between these two factors, as shown in Table 5.7. This result is different from that of Study I. In Study I, 32 of the 37 participants (86%) in the DTG who increased their scores in Week 15 were low-intermediate listeners, and there was significance in the interaction between 'more/less than 250 in Week 1' and 'before/after the study' at the 1% level. The results of Study I indicate that specific training that focuses on phonetic level, such as dictation training, is more effective for low-intermediate listeners. Table 5.23 presents the score proportion in Week 1 of the DTG participants whose scores increased in Week 15 of both Studies I and III.

Table 5.23 Score Proportion of the DTG Participants whose Scores Increased in Week 15 of Studies I and III

	Dictation Training	
	Less than 250 in Week 1	250 or more in Week 1
Study I	86%	14%
Study III	44%	56%

Although dictation training was significantly effective in the both studies, the majority of these increased scores in Week 15 differed in Studies I and III. One possible reason for this phenomenon might be that the proficiency level of the DTG participants in Study I was lower than that of the DTG participants in Study III (Table 5.24). Although all the participants in the studies were at the intermediate level, there were more low-intermediate listeners in Study I, whereas there were more upper-intermediate listeners in Study III. This might be the reason for such differences.

Table 5.24 Comparison of the DTG Participants in Studies I and III

	Week 1			Week 15			
	N	Mean	SD	Mean	SD	Relative Value	Mean of difference
Study I DTG	52	230.19	28.90	253.46	37.02	1.10	23.27
Study III DTG	34	241.91	39.16	268.82	47.26	1.11	26.91

Study III - Dictation Training and Listening Strategy Training with the MALQ

Now, let us focus on the LSTG participants who increased their scores in Week 15. Figure 5.5 shows that 25 of the 37 participants (67%) in the LSTG increased their scores in Week 15, and 21 of the 25 participants (84%) were low-intermediate listeners (Figure 5.6). The majority of those in the LSTG who increased their scores in Week 15 were low-intermediate listeners, and the same results were observed in Study I. Table 5.25 presents the score proportion in Week 1 of the LSTG participants whose scores increased in Week 15 of both Studies I and III.

Table 5.25   Score Proportion of the LSTG Participants whose Scores Increased in Week 15 of Studies I and III

	Listening Strategy Training	
	Less than 250 in Week 1	250 or more in Week 1
Study I	59%	41%
Study III	84%	16%

A two-way ANOVA was conducted for further analysis on two factors, i.e. 'more/less than 250 in Week 1' and 'before/after the study'. The results show that there was significance in the interaction between these two factors at the 0.1% level, as shown in Table 5.8. The simple main effect test about listening strategy training also showed significance between the 14 upper- and 23 low-intermediate listeners based on their scores of the listening parts of the TOEIC® in Week 1. These results indicate that listening strategy training is significantly effective, especially for *upper*-intermediate listeners at the 0.1% level (Table 5.10). Although listening strategy training was significantly effective in both the studies, significance in the interaction between two factors (i.e. 'more/less than 250 in Week 1' and 'before/after the study') was only obtained in Study III. One possible reason for this might be the difference in the SD since other factors in Studies I and III are similar, except for the number of the participants. In

Study I, the SD of the LSTG is 45.19, whereas it is 30.88 in Study III (Table 5.26). This finding indicates that the spread of the distribution in Study I was much more than that of Study III. In addition, it is assumed that a smaller SD probably contributes to significance and this assumption is supported by other data. Although dictation training was significantly effective in both studies, significance in the interaction between the two factors (i.e. 'more/less than 250 in Week 1' and 'before/after the study') was only found in Study I. Table 5.27 shows the summary of significance regarding the two teaching methods in Studies I and III. Table 5.24 shows that the SD of the DTG is 37.02 in Study I, whereas it is 47.26 in Study III. These results prove that significance is observed in studies where the SD is less than 40. Thus, it is considered that the smaller SD probably contributes to significance.

Table 5.26 Comparison of the LSTG Participants in Studies I and III

	Week 1			Week 15			
	N	Mean	SD	Mean	SD	Relative Value	Mean of difference
Study I LSTG	46	241.30	32.41	263.26	45.19	1.09	21.96
Study III LSTG	37	242.84	32.22	264.19	30.88	1.09	21.35

Table 5.27 Summary of Significance about the Teaching Methods in Studies I and III

	Dictation Training		Listening Strategy Training	
	Less than 250 in Week 1	250 or more in Week 1	Less than 250 in Week 1	250 or more in Week 1
Study I	significant			
Study III				significant

Table 5.28 presents the summary regarding the percentages of those who increased their scores in dictation training and listening strategy training in Studies I and III, respectively. Although the difference is not significant, it is clear that more participants in the DTG increased their scores than the

LSTG in both the studies. Based on the theories of both Schneider and Shiffrin (1977) and Anderson (2010), these results are logical and reasonable, and specific listening training that focuses on phonetic level, such as dictation training, can enhance the level of perception in listeners, which ultimately leads them to higher levels (i.e. parsing and utilisation).

Table 5.28   Comparison of Those who Increased and Decreased Their Scores in the DTG and LSTGI n Studies I and III[18]

	Dictation Training		Listening Strategy Training	
	Increased	Decreased	Increased	Decreased
Study I	71%	23%	70%	28%
Study III	79%	21%	67%	30%

5.4.4 Discussion about the DTG and LSTG participants whose scores decreased in Week 15

In Study III, both dictation training and listening strategy training were statistically effective for intermediate listeners under a certain condition (in this case, 30 minutes for 13 weeks). Whilst the majority of the participants in both groups increased their scores in Week 15, many participants in both groups decreased their scores in Week 15.

First, let us investigate the DTG. Figure 5.3 shows that seven of the 34 participants (21%) in the DTG decreased their scores in Week 15, and five of these seven participants (71%) were upper-intermediate listeners (Figure 5.7). In Study I, 12 of the 52 DTG participants (23%) decreased their scores in Week 15, and six of the 12 participants (50%) were upper-intermediate listeners (Figures 3.3 and 3.7). After comparing Figures 5.4 and 5.7, it was found that upper-intermediate listeners are more likely to decrease their scores with dictation training. Although it does not exceed more than 50% in Study I, the same result was obtained in Study I (Figure 3.7). One possible

---

[18] Some participants did not change their scores before and after the study; 6% in the DTG, 2% in the LSTG in Study I and 3% in the LSTG in Study III.

reason for this could be explained by the score of 250 in the listening parts of the TOEIC®. Those who achieved the TOEIC® listening scores of 250 or more in Week 1 might have overcome the level of perception, the lowest level in Anderson's (2010) cognitive psychology theory. Thus, basic phonetic perception training, such as dictation training, might no longer be effective for those who have passed this level. This assumption and the results are consistent with the theories of Schneider and Shiffrin (1977) and Anderson (2010).

Table 5.29 Score Proportion of the DTG Participants whose Scores Decreased in Week 15 of Studies I and III

	Dictation Training	
	Less than 250 in Week 1	250 or more in Week 1
Study I	50%	50%
Study III	29%	71%

Now, let us observe the LSTG. Figures 5.5 and 5.8 show that 11 of the 37 LSTG participants (30%) decreased their scores in Week 15, and nine of these 11 participants (82%) were upper-intermediate listeners (Table 5.30 below). After comparing Figures 5.6 and 5.8, upper-intermediate listeners are more likely to decrease their scores, which was the same finding as in Study I. Table 5.30 presents the score proportion in Week 1 of the LSTG participants whose scores decreased in Week 15 of both Studies I and III.

Table 5.30 Score Proportion of the LSTG Participants whose Scores Decreased in Week 15 of Studies I and III

	Listening Strategy Training	
	Less than 250 in Week 1	250 or more in Week 1
Study I	46%	54%
Study III	18%	82%

Although it has been proven that the effect of listening strategy training between low- and upper-intermediate listeners is significant at the 0.1% level (Table 5.8), why is listening strategy training ineffective for some upper-intermediate listeners? As proven thus far, if those with TOEIC® listening scores of 250 or more in Week 1 have overcome the level of perception, then theoretically, listening strategy training could be effective specifically for upper-intermediate listeners. What is the difference between those who increased and decreased their scores amongst the upper-intermediate listeners? In the following section, this question is investigated and discussed based on the data from the MALQ.

5.4.5 Discussion about the MALQ

In this section, the results of the MALQ, which was conducted for all the three groups in both Weeks 1 and 15, are analysed and discussed from a different perspective: metacognitive awareness before and after the study. In addition, the results of the MALQ in Studies II and III are compared and discussed. The discussion is as per the following five factors by comparing the differences in the CG, DTG and LSTG before and after the study. Only the items whose difference is 0.5 or more are closely analysed since the difference below 0.5 is considered as nil in this study.

1) Directed Attention; ways of concentrating on certain aspects of a task
2) Mental Translation; translation from English to L1 when listening
3) Person Knowledge;
   confidence or anxiety and self-perception as a listener
4) Planning and Evaluation; preparing to listen and assessing success
5) Problem Solving; guessing as well as monitoring these guesses

First, there are four items that investigate Directed Attention in the MALQ:

No. 2: I focus harder on the text when I have trouble understanding.
No. 6: When my mind wanders, I recover my concentration right away.
No.12: I try to get back on track when I lose concentration.
No. 16: When I have difficulty understanding what I hear, I give up and stop listening.

Table 5.31   Differences in the Post-Mean Scores in the CG, DTG and LSTG about Directed Attention

Directed Attention	2			6			12			16		
	CG	DTG	LSTG	CG	DTG	LSTG	CG	DTG	LSTG	CG	DTG	LSTG
Wk 1	4.3	4.8	4.2	3.9	4.3	4.5	4.2	4.3	4.5	3.3	3.0	3.2
Wk 15	3.8	4.7	4.4	4.2	4.6	4.8	4.2	4.5	4.8	3.5	2.8	2.5
D	-0.5	-0.1	0.2	0.3	0.3	0.3	0	0.2	0.3	0.2	-0.2	-0.7

Scale

1	2	3	4	5	6
Strongly disagree	Disagree	Slightly disagree	Partly agree	Agree	Strongly agree

According to Table 5.31, No. 2 in the CG shows a change of 0.5, which does not represent an improvement in metacognitive awareness since the post-mean score is within the range of 3 (Slightly disagree) (Figure 5.9 and Table 5.11). The same result was obtained in Study II in which the CG participants showed no improvement in Directed Attention in metacognition. Based on these results, it is assumed that Directed Attention does not improve if intermediate listeners do not receive special listening training. In addition, they continue having difficulty concentrating and tend to stop listening when facing difficulty in listening in English.

Now, let us observe the results of the DTG. All the items show a change of no more than 0.3 (Figure 5.10 and Tables 5.12 and 5.31). Again, the results show that dictation training, under the conditions of Study III, has no effect for intermediate listeners to improve Directed Attention in metacognition. Similar to their CG counterparts, they also continue having difficulty concentrating, and also tend to stop listening when facing difficulty in listening in English.

Next, let us analyse the results of the LSTG. The post-mean scores of Nos. 2, 6 and 12 show a change of no more than 0.3 (Figure 5.11 and Tables 5.13 and 5.31). Although No. 16 in the LSTG shows a decrease of 0.7 from 3.2 (Slightly disagree) to 2.5, it actually represents an improvement since the post-mean score changed to the range of 2 (Disagree) for the item: When I have difficulty understanding what I hear, I give up and stop listening. Since No. 16 is the only sign of improvement in Directed Attention in metacognition, these results show that listening strategy training, under the conditions of Study III, does not seem to be extremely effective for intermediate listeners on Directed Attention.

Second, there are three items that investigate Mental Translation in the MALQ:

No. 4:   I translate in my head as I listen.
No.11:   I translate key words as I listen.
No.18:   I translate word by word as I listen.[19]

Table 5.32   Differences in the Post-Mean Scores in the CG, DTG and LSTG about Mental Translation

Mental Translation	4			11			18		
	CG	DTG	LSTG	CG	DTG	LSTG	CG	DTG	LSTG
Wk 1	4.0	3.8	3.8	4.0	4.0	4.3	4.0	4.0	2.4
Wk 15	3.8	3.7	3.3	4.3	3.9	4.1	4.3	3.9	1.9
D	-0.2	-0.1	-0.5	0.3	-0.1	-0.2	0.3	-0.1	-0.5

---

[19] sic

Scale

1	2	3	4	5	6
Strongly disagree	Disagree	Slightly disagree	Partly agree	Agree	Strongly agree

Table 5.32 shows that all the items in the CG show a change of no more than 0.3. The results indicate that the CG participants showed no improvement regarding Mental Translation in metacognition. Based on these results, it is assumed that Mental Translation does not improve when intermediate listeners do not receive special listening training since they continue translating the presented material.

However, this result differs from that of Study II. In Study II, intermediate listeners translated the information with less frequency even when they did not receive any special listening training. This might be due to the EFL listening proficiency differences between the CG participants in Studies II and III. In fact, the proficiency level in the EFL listening of the CG participants in Study II was higher (Tables 4.4 and 5.3). Thus, intermediate listeners who do not receive listening training have a tendency to translate many words, including key words. However, depending on their proficiency level, they may be able to translate the presented material with less frequency.

Now, let us observe the results of the DTG. Table 5.32 shows that all the items in the DTG show almost no difference. Like the CG, the results show that dictation training, under the conditions of Study III, has no effect for improving intermediate listeners' Directed Attention in metacognition: They continue translating the presented material.

Next, let us analyse the results of the LSTG. Table 5.32 shows that the post-mean scores of Nos. 4 and 18 in the LSTG decreased by 0.5, respectively. However, it does not represent the deterioration of Mental Translation. In fact, it is an improvement. For example, let us look at No. 18: I translate word by word, as I listen. Before the study, the mean score of the

LSTG participants was 2.4 (Disagree). However, after the study, it changed to 1.9 (Strongly disagree). Although No. 11 does not show prominent change, this result might indicate that listening strategy training, under the conditions of Study III, has a certain degree of influence for intermediate listeners to improve Mental Translation in metacognition: They can gradually decrease their tendency to translate the presented material.

Third, there are three items that investigate Person Knowledge in the MALQ:

No. 3: I find that listening is more difficult than reading, speaking, or writing in English.
No. 8: I feel that listening comprehension in English is a challenge for me.
No.15: I don't[20] feel nervous when I listen to English.

Table 5.33   Differences in the Post-Mean Scores in the CG, DTG and LSTG about Person Knowledge

Person Knowledge	3			8			15		
	CG	DTG	LSTG	CG	DTG	LSTG	CG	DTG	LSTG
Wk 1	4.1	3.3	3.3	3.6	4.7	4.4	1.8	2.3	1.9
Wk 15	4.7	3.6	3.5	4.0	4.6	4.8	2.0	2.1	2.3
D	0.6	0.3	0.2	0.4	-0.1	0.4	0.2	-0.2	0.4

Scale

1	2	3	4	5	6
Strongly disagree	Disagree	Slightly disagree	Partly agree	Agree	Strongly agree

According to Table 5.33, none of the post-mean scores in the CG changed by more than 0.5 except for No. 3. In regard to No. 3, although it changed from 4.1 to 4.7, it still remained within the range of 4 (Partly agree) for the item: I find that listening is more difficult than reading, speaking, or writing

---

[20] sic

in English. Based on these results, it is assumed that Person Knowledge in metacognition does not seem to improve when intermediate listeners do not receive special listening training. The same result was obtained in Study II where intermediate listeners without special listening training remained nervous and found listening in English challenging.

Now, let us observe the results of the DTG. Table 5.33 shows that all the items in the DTG show a change of no more than 0.5. Like the CG, the results indicate that dictation training, under the conditions of Study III, has no effect for intermediate listeners to improve Person Knowledge in metacognition: Intermediate listeners remain nervous and find listening in English challenging.

Next, let us observe the results of the LSTG. According to Table 5.33, all the items in the LSTG show a change of no more than 0.5. Like the CG and DTG, the results show that listening strategy training, under the conditions of Study III, has no effect for intermediate listeners to improve Person Knowledge in metacognition: Intermediate listeners remain nervous and find listening in English challenging.

Fourth, there are five items that investigate Planning/Evaluation in the MALQ:

No. 1: Before I start to listen, I have a plan in my head for how I am going to listen.
No. 10: Before listening, I think of similar texts that I may have listened to.
No. 14: After listening, I think back to how I listened, and about what I might do differently next time.
No. 20: As I listen, I periodically ask myself if I am satisfied with my level of comprehension.
No. 21: I have a goal in mind as I listen.

Table 5.34 Differences in the Post-Mean Scores in the CG, DTG and LSTG about Planning/Evaluation

Planning Evaluation	1			10			14			20			21		
	CG	DTG	LSTG	CG	DTG	LSTG	CG	DTG	LSTG	CG	DTG	LSTG	CG	DTG	LSTG
Wk 1	3.9	3.9	4.3	3.4	4.3	3.8	3.1	3.8	3.7	2.6	3.5	3.4	3.8	4.5	4.2
Wk 15	4.2	4.3	4.9	3.7	4.3	4.7	4.0	3.7	4.3	3.3	3.3	3.3	4.3	4.3	4.7
D	0.3	0.4	0.6	0.3	0	0.9	0.9	-0.1	0.6	0.7	-0.2	-0.1	0.5	-0.2	0.5

Scale

1	2	3	4	5	6
Strongly disagree	Disagree	Slightly disagree	Partly agree	Agree	Strongly agree

Table 5.34 reveals that the post-mean scores of the CG in Nos. 14, 20 and 21 show a change of 0.5 or more. As for No. 14, it changed from 3.1 (Slightly disagree) to 4.0 (Partly agree) for the item: After listening, I think back to how I listened, and about what I might do differently next time. As for No. 21, it changed from 3.8 (Slightly disagree) to 4.3 (Partly agree) for the item: I have a goal in mind as I listen. Based on these two items, intermediate listeners seem to improve planning/evaluation without any special listening training. However, Nos. 1 and 10 show no change of more than 0.5. In addition, the post-mean score of No. 20 still remains within the range of 3 (Disagree) for the item: As I listen, I periodically ask myself if I am satisfied with my level of comprehension. These results indicate that Planning/Evaluation in metacognition does not generally improve without any particular listening training. The same result was obtained in Study II.

Now, let us investigate the DTG. Table 5.34 demonstrates that none of the post-mean scores of the DTG changed by more than 0.5. Based on these results, it is assumed that dictation training, under the conditions of Study III, has no effect for intermediate listeners to improve Planning/Evaluation in metacognition: Intermediate listeners were unable to plan how they were going to listen and evaluate how they listened with dictation training under the conditions of Study III.

Next, let us analyse the results of the LSTG. Table 5.34 shows that all the items, except for No. 20, show a change of 0.5 or more. These results indicate that listening strategy training, under the conditions of Study III, is effective for intermediate listeners to improve Planning/Evaluation in metacognition: They can gain the ability to plan how they are going to listen, think of similar texts before listening, evaluate how they listened and have a goal in mind when listening in English.

Finally, there are six items that investigate Problem Solving in the MALQ:

No. 5: I use the words I understand to guess the meaning of words I don't[21] understand.
No. 7: As I listen, I compare what I understand with what I know about the topic.
No. 9: I use my experience and knowledge to help me understand.
No. 13: As I listen, I quickly adjust my interpretation if I realise that it is not correct.
No. 17: I use the general idea of the text to help me guess the meaning of words that I don't[22] understand.
No. 19: When I guess the meaning of a word, I think back to everything that I have heard,[23] to see if my guess makes sense.

---

[21] sic
[22] sic
[23] sic

Table 5.35　Differences in the Post-Mean Scores in the CG, DTG and LSTG about Problem Solving

Problem Solving	5			7			9			13			17			19		
	CG	DTG	LSTG	CG	DTG	LSTG	CG	DTG	LSTG	CG	DTG	LSTG	CG	DTG	LSTG	CG	DTG	LSTG
Wk 1	4.0	4.7	4.0	3.4	4.3	4.2	4.3	4.7	4.7	4.1	4.2	4.1	3.8	4.3	4.0	3.9	4.5	4.2
Wk 15	4.0	4.6	4.7	3.8	4.1	4.9	4.5	4.6	5.4	4.6	4.2	4.8	4.1	4.5	4.8	4.1	4.5	4.7
D	0	-0.1	0.7	0.4	-0.2	0.7	0.2	-0.1	0.7	0.5	0	0.7	0.3	0.2	0.8	0.2	0	0.5

Scale

1	2	3	4	5	6
Strongly disagree	Disagree	Slightly disagree	Partly agree	Agree	Strongly agree

Table 5.35 indicates that the CG shows no change of more than 0.5. These results indicate that intermediate listeners are unable to improve Problem Solving in metacognition without any particular listening training. The same result was obtained in Study II.

The same features are observed in the DTG. No item shows a change of more than 0.5. These results indicate that dictation training, under the conditions of Study III, has no effect for intermediate listeners to improve Problem Solving in metacognition.

Now, let us observe the results of the LSTG. Every item shows an increase of 0.5 or more. These results show that listening strategy training, under the conditions of Study III, is effective for intermediate listeners to improve Problem Solving in metacognition: With listening strategy training, intermediate listeners can possibly gain the ability to guess the meaning of unknown words by thinking back to everything that they have heard, using the general idea of the text, comparing what they understand with what they know about the topic, using their experience and knowledge and monitoring their comprehension and adjusting it if necessary.

In Study II, dictation training and listening strategy training were combined, and consequently, it was difficult to judge which training was more effective. However, Study III shows that listening strategy has a distinctive effect specifically on Problem Solving in metacognition.

Thus far, the features and changes regarding the metacognitive skills of the participants in the CG, DTG and LSTG have been observed and discussed. Finally, let us briefly observe those in both the DTG and LSTG who increased their scores for further investigation that focuses only on changes of more than 1.0 between the pre- and post-mean scores on the MALQ. Figure 5.12 and Tables 5.16 and 5.22 show that the top 10 DTG participants made no change of more than 1.0 in all the items.

As for the LSTG, the top 12 participants show a change (Figure 5.14, Tables 5.20 and 5.22) of 1.2 in No. 10 (planning/evaluation) from 3.8 (Slightly disagree) to 5.0 (Agree) for the item: Before listening, I think of similar texts that I may have listened to. As stated earlier, the most prominent difference amongst the CG, DTG and LSTG is that the LSTG participants improved most of their metacognitive skills in both Planning/Evaluation and Problem Solving. Based on these results, it can be concluded that an improvement of Planning/Evaluation and Problem Solving in metacognitive skills is the key to becoming an effective listener. Overall, it has become clear that the ability to tackle problems when listening with various strategies, including grammar, background knowledge, inference, vocabulary, planning, monitoring one's comprehension and evaluation, are vital for 'survival' in EFL listening. This is similar to the concept in which only creatures with diversity can evolve and survive over the long term.

5.5 Summary

S-1 Both dictation training and listening strategy training are significantly effective for intermediate listeners.

S-2 Listening strategy training is significantly effective, especially for upper-intermediate listeners.

Study III - Dictation Training and Listening Strategy Training with the MALQ

S-3 Without special listening training, intermediate listeners do not improve metacognitive skills in EFL listening.

S-4 Dictation training is not effective for intermediate listeners to improve metacognitive skills in EFL listening.

S-5 Listening strategy training is effective for intermediate listeners to improve some metacognitive skills in EFL listening such as Mental Translation, Planning/Evaluation and Problem Solving.

S-6 The improvement of Planning/Evaluation and Problem Solving in metacognitive skills is vital for becoming an advanced listener in EFL listening.

    A total of 94 Japanese learners of English participated in Study III. Only those who scored between 166 and 330 in the listening parts of the TOEIC® in Week 1 were selected after which they were divided into three groups, i.e. the CG, DTG and LSTG. There were 23, 34 and 37 participants in the CG, DTG and LSTG, respectively. During Weeks 2 and 14, the CG participants had no training except for their usual 90-minute class each week. The DTG participants received dictation training for 30 minutes in their usual 90-minute class each week, whereas the LSTG participants were instructed on the various types of listening strategies for 30 minutes in their usual 90-minute class each week. In Week 15, all the participants took the same listening parts of the TOEIC® as in Week 1.

    The results show that 79% of the DTG participants and 67% of the LSTG participants increased their scores in Week 15 and that significance was observed in their increases of both the DTG and LSTG with a two-way ANOVA. The same results were obtained in Study I. Like Study I, based on the idea that the score range of 166–330 in the listening parts of the TOEIC® is probably very broad to withdraw a concrete result, the DTG and

LSTG participants were further divided into two groups, i.e. low-intermediate listeners (who scored less than 250 in the listening part of the TOEIC® in Week 1) and upper-intermediate listeners (who scored 250 or more on the same test). In the DTG, no significance was obtained between low- and upper-intermediate listeners of dictation training, whereas significant effectiveness of listening strategy training was found for the upper-intermediate listeners.

Finally, the results show that intermediate listeners do not improve metacognitive skills in EFL listening without any special listening training, that dictation training is not effective for them to improve metacognitive skills in EFL listening and that listening strategy training is effective for improving some metacognitive skills in EFL listening such as Mental Translation, Planning/Evaluation and Problem Solving. Based on the features on the MALQ of those who increased their scores in the listening parts of the TOEIC® in Week 15, it is concluded that an improvement of Planning/Evaluation in metacognitive skills is vital for becoming an advanced listener in EFL listening. The importance of the explicit teaching of second language listening in the language classroom is supported by Vandergrift and Goh (2009) who found that such instruction has often been neglected and left to be incidentally developed through tasks that focus on other language skills.

Chapter 6: Summary, Implications and Suggestions

The purpose of this chapter is threefold. First, it attempts to provide a summary of the studies conducted in this study and a synopsis of the results. Second, it describes the implications of the study. Finally, it offers some suggestions for future research.

6.1 Overview of the Studies

The goals of this study were to investigate the effective teaching methods in EFL listening, especially for intermediate levels, and to appeal the importance of using a standardised test in any EFL/ESL research. For these goals, the following seven hypotheses were investigated based on the listening parts of the TOEIC® and the MALQ:

H-1 For intermediate listeners, dictation training is more effective than listening strategy training.

H-2 For low-intermediate listeners, dictation training is more effective.

H-3 For intermediate listeners, the combined training of dictation and listening strategy is not effective for improving EFL listening comprehension.

H-4 For intermediate listeners, the combined training of dictation and listening strategy is not significantly effective for improving metacognitive skills in EFL listening.

H-5   For intermediate listeners, both dictation training and listening strategy training are effective with significance.

H-6   For upper-intermediate listeners, listening strategy training is more effective.

H-7   Intermediate listeners with listening strategy training show a greater change in their metacognitive skills.

To test these hypotheses, three studies were conducted (i.e. Studies I, II and III). The purpose of Study I was to investigate Hypotheses 1 and 2. The participants consisted of 108 first-year students (in the Faculty of Economics) at a Japanese private university. Only those who scored between 166 and 330 in the listening parts of the TOEIC® were selected and divided into three groups (i.e. CG, DTG and LSTG) in Week 1. From Weeks 2 to 14, for 30 minutes in their usual weekly class for 13 weeks, the DTG participants received dictation training, whereas the LSTG participants received training in the various types of listening strategies. In Week 15, the same listening parts of the TOEIC® were used to investigate Hypotheses 1 and 2.

The purpose of Study II was to investigate Hypotheses 3 and 4. The participants consisted of 57 first-year students (in the Faculty of Economics) at a Japanese private university. Only those who scored between 166 and 330 in the listening parts of the TOEIC® were selected and divided into two groups (i.e. CG and D+LSTG) in Week 1. The MALQ was also administered in Week 1 in order to examine the participants' metacognitive awareness in EFL listening before the study. From Weeks 2 to 14, for 60 minutes in their usual weekly class for 13 weeks, the D+LSTG participants received the combined training of both dictation training and the various types of listening strategies. In Week 15, the same listening parts of the TOEIC® and MALQ were used to investigate Hypotheses 3 and 4.

The purpose of Study III was to investigate Hypotheses 5, 6 and 7. The participants consisted of 94 first-year students (in the Faculty of Economics) at a Japanese private university. Only those who scored between 166 and 330 in the listening parts of the TOEIC® were selected and divided into three groups (i.e. CG, DTG and LSTG) in Week 1. The MALQ was also administered in Week 1 to examine the participants' metacognitive awareness in EFL listening before the study. From Weeks 2 to 14, for 30 minutes in their usual weekly class for 13 weeks, the DTG participants received dictation training, whereas the LSTG participants received training in the various types of listening strategies. In Week 15, the same listening parts of the TOEIC® and the MALQ were used to investigate Hypotheses 5, 6 and 7.

In each study, a two-way ANOVA was conducted, and the effect size was measured using each participant's score of the listening parts of the TOEIC® (before and after the study) in order to examine the effect of each training. In addition, Ryan's method was employed to trace where the significance lies when the result of the ANOVA was significant. For a deeper investigation, the participants were divided into two groups, i.e. lower- and upper-intermediate listeners. The former consisted of participants who scored less than 250 in the listening parts of the TOEIC® in Week 1, whereas the latter consisted of those who scored 250 or more in the same test.

6.2 Overview of the Findings

The three studies provided the results necessary to investigate the seven aforementioned hypotheses. The results of Study I revealed that 71% of the DTG participants and 70% of the LSTG participants increased their scores in Week 15, that both dictation training and listening strategy training were significantly effective for intermediate listeners and that dictation training was significantly effective specifically for low-intermediate listeners. These results supported Hypotheses 1 and 2.

Study II showed that the combined training of dictation training and listening strategy training was not effective for intermediate listeners, that the combined listening training was not effective for intermediate listeners to improve some metacognitive skills in EFL listening such as Directed Attention, Mental Translation, and Person Knowledge and that an improvement of Planning/Evaluation and Problem Solving in metacognitive skills were vital to becoming an advanced listener in EFL listening. These findings confirmed Hypotheses 3 and 4.

The results of Study III revealed that 79% of the DTG participants and 67% of the LSTG participants increased their scores in Week 15. In addition, the findings showed that both dictation training and listening strategy training were significantly effective for intermediate listeners, that listening strategy training was significantly effective for upper-intermediate listeners, that intermediate listeners did not improve metacognitive skills in EFL listening without any listening training, that dictation training was not effective for intermediate listeners to improve metacognitive skills in EFL listening, that listening strategy training was effective for intermediate listeners to improve some metacognitive skills in EFL listening such as Mental Translation, Planning/Evaluation and Problem Solving and that an improvement of both Planning/Evaluation and Problem Solving in metacognitive skills was vital to becoming an advanced listener in EFL listening. Therefore, Hypotheses 5, 6 and 7 were all confirmed.

Finally, all the results in Studies I, II and III confirmed the theories of both Schneider and Shiffrin (1977) and Anderson (2010), in which there are gradual steps in both human information processing and language comprehension.

6.3 Implications of the Study

As stated in Chapter 2, numerous studies on EFL/ESL listening strategies have been conducted within the framework of applied linguistics and cognitive psychology since the 1970s (Brown, 1977; DeFilippis, 1980;

O'Malley, Chamot and Küpper, 1989; Vandergrift, 1997; Goh, 2000; Graham, Santos and Vanderplank, 2011). The majority of these studies have concluded that advanced listeners use a wide array of listening strategies and that teaching listening strategies is effective. However, many of these studies neither employed a standardised test to measure the proficiency level of the participants before and after the studies nor clearly defined how the participants were categorised. Without making these two points objectively clear, no scientific results are expected and no solid outcome is gained, regardless of the field. Therefore, the present study was undertaken to address these shortcomings. The findings of this study significantly contribute to the field of EFL listening, as described in the following paragraphs.

The most important contribution of this investigation is the confirmation that dictation training is significantly effective for low-intermediate listeners and that listening strategy training is also significantly effective for upper-intermediate listeners. This sheds new light on the study of EFL listening. By examining the level of listening competence in English with a standardised test *prior to* the training, it is possible for both instructors and learners to know which type of training is more effective for learners. Many Japanese learners of English have been repeatedly instructed to 'listen again' and to 'listen carefully', but there are many situations in which learners cannot comprehend what is being said, regardless of their attempts to listen. Thus, learners need to know where comprehension breaks down, its cause and diagnostic instructions.

To begin with, dictation is probably the best way to investigate where comprehension breaks down. By comparing what is dictated with the audio script, it is possible to check the perception level. It is not necessary to dictate every single word but focus on whether only content words are written down. If any content word is missing at this level, then the possible causes are 1) the learner does not know the word, 2) the learner knows the word but does not know its spelling and 3) the learner can recognise the word by reading but not simply by listening. Vocabulary study can be instructed for the first and the second cases. For the third case, however, the three steps in dictation training procedure described in this study can be suggested.

When there is no problem in the perception level, the level of parsing can be checked by inserting slashes on the audio script. If they are inserted at grammatically incorrect places, the possible remedy is to instruct grammar in English.

Finally, when there is no problem in the parsing level, the level of utilisation can be checked by either translating the sentences or rephrasing them in English. For example, a sentence such as 'Were you born in a barn?' does not actually enquire whether the listener was born in a barn, as discussed in Chapter 2. The possible causes at this level are lack of background knowledge and/or inference. Thus, a potential instruction would provide the knowledge and further information about it. Hence, diagnostic instructions in listening with Anderson's (2010) theory are possible at a classroom level.

As for the importance of diagnostic instructions in listening, Sheerin (1987, p. 129) indicates that until we have some diagnostic procedures, teachers can only continue to *test* comprehension but not teach it. Mendelsohn (1995, p. 133) also argues that the task of language teachers is to teach students how to listen by using strategies that will ultimately lead to better comprehension rather than merely giving students an opportunity to listen.

The present study can provide both instructors and learners with insights where understanding has broken down based on the theory of Anderson (2010). These insights can be followed up with small-scale remedial exercises that can help prevent the errors of interpretation (especially low-level errors) from occurring again (Field, 2003, p. 326). Most people have limited time and money, and under these conditions, it is natural that one seeks the most effective way to reach a certain goal. Thus, providing more effective teaching or learning methods for particular learners would be greatly beneficial.

The second contribution of this study is to focus on the intermediate level. From empirical research perspective, it is natural for researchers to choose advanced learners and less-advanced learners since the gap between these two groups is generally large and easy to compare. However, intermediate learners make up the majority of the population, as proven in Chapter 1. Examples include this author's classes in which 99% of the students were intermediate listeners based on their scores of the listening parts of the TOEIC® in 2014 (Figure 1.4). Not only in this author's classes but also the majority of Asian and South American learners of English are categorised as intermediate in listening (Figure 1.8). The findings of the present study, which only focuses on intermediate listeners, can provide detailed insight into the formulation of future research designs on EFL/ESL listening.

The third contribution of this study is the introduction of a standardised test with a clear definition regarding how the participants were divided. As stated in Chapter 2, some researchers agree that listening strategy training is effective in EFL/ESL, whereas others disagree. One of the main reasons for this disagreement could be derived from the lack of a standardised test in these studies. Without the use of such a test, those categorised as more-successful listeners in one study might be considered as intermediate in another, whilst those categorised as intermediate in one study might be classified as less successful in another. Regardless of the outcomes of these studies, it would be extremely difficult or sometimes impossible to compare the results with those of other studies without such a test. In addition, regardless of how many studies are conducted, the research of EFL/ESL listening would not be fruitful. Although Rubin (1994) indicated this important issue 20 years earlier, many studies have still been conducted without a standardised test. Moreover, it is essential to clearly describe how the participants were divided or categorised in a study. In this study, the listening parts of the TOEIC® were used as the standardised test and only those who scored between 166 and 330 were selected as intermediate listeners. Therefore, the results of this study can be easily adapted to many EFL/ESL learners by using Table 2.3 in Chapter 2. Although the listening parts of the TOEIC® were used as the standardised test in this study, it is not necessary to use this test as the standardised test. Any language proficiency test, which is reliable, international, popular, relatively easy to access and capable of comparing/converting other tests, can be used as a standardised test.

The final contribution of this study is in regard to metacognition in EFL listening. As stated in Chapter 2, an improvement in metacognitive skills in EFL/ESL is not doubtful. In addition, the findings from Studies II and III provide a concrete pedagogical implication. An improvement of Planning/Evaluation and Problem Solving in metacognitive skills is vital to become an advanced listener in EFL listening. More specifically, Nos. 1, 10, 14, 20 and 21 for Planning/Evaluation and Nos. 5, 7, 9, 13, 17 and 19 in the MALQ for Problem Solving can provide aspects regarding what learners should be aware of. The results of this study prove that it is possible to determine which type of training is more effective for learners based on their scores of the listening parts of the TOEIC® *prior to* the training. At the same time, being aware of improving Planning/Evaluation and Problem Solving in metacognitive skills is vital

and extremely beneficial to become an advanced listener in EFL listening.

6.4 Suggestions for Future Research

The present study investigated the effect of teaching methods for EFL intermediate listeners. In this study, particular emphasis was placed on the intermediate level. Therefore, this experimental study can be replicated and extended in several directions.

First, it would be interesting to replicate this study with different linguistic backgrounds in Asia and South America. As stated in Chapter 2, it has been proven that the majority of learners of English in Asia and South

America are at the intermediate level. This study identified that dictation training is significantly effective for low-intermediate listeners, that listening strategy training is significantly effective for upper-intermediate listeners and that an improvement of both Planning/Evaluation and Problem Solving in metacognitive skills is vital to become an advanced listener in EFL listening. However, it would be interesting to determine if the same results can be obtained with EFL/ESL learners in Asia and South America.

Second, the results can be supplemented by a different combination of the two types of training, i.e. dictation training and listening strategy training. Although the results of this study confirmed that the combined training of dictation training and listening strategy training was not significantly effective for intermediate listeners, it would be interesting to investigate the effect of a different combination of training. For example, for one group, dictation training could be given for 60 minutes a week (from Weeks 2 to 7) for six weeks, and then listening strategy training could be conducted for 60 minutes a week (from Weeks 9 to 14) for another six weeks. For another group, listening strategy training could be given for 60 minutes a week (Weeks 2 to 7) for six weeks and dictation training could be conducted for 60 minutes a week (Weeks 9 to 14) for another six weeks. In Weeks 1, 8 and 15, a pre-, mid and post-tests, could be conducted, respectively with a standardised test. The unique feature of this suggested study is that there is no control group in general. To make an empirical study objective and scientific, it is impossible to avoid having a control group. However, some researchers find it unethical. For us instructors, we *do* know that the participants in a control group receive no benefit from the research even before it begins. A control group is vital as a researcher, but it might be unprincipled as an instructor. With the style of the suggested study above, it is not necessary to have a control group even in an empirical study. Thus, the suggested study is unique due to this feature.

Finally, even if a research result shows that a certain teaching method is effective, it is not scientific to make conclusions based on a single research result. In addition, when the method is taught by another instructor, the results might be different. To expect the same effect, an appropriate competence or working knowledge of the teaching methods is vital, and such competence or knowledge can only be based on the judgement of the instructor in the classroom. Instructors must pay careful attention to their students, whether they are following the given instructions, when employing the teaching methods. Thus, an effective teaching method and an appropriate competence or working knowledge of the teaching methods should work in cooperation.

For many years, Japanese learners of English have been simply instructed to 'listen carefully' and 'listen many times', and then *tested* on their comprehension level in EFL/ESL listening. However, 'listening test' and 'listening instruction' are two different things. Instructors should instruct '*how*' to teach listening', or where comprehension breaks down, why comprehension breaks down and how to address problems in EFL/ESL listening before *testing*.

References

Aaronson, D., & Scarborough, H. S. (1977). Performance theories for sentence coding: Some quantitative models. *Journal of Verbal Learning and Verbal Behavior, 16,* 277-304.

American Psychological Association. (2001). *Publication Manual of the American Psychological Association,* 5th ed. Washington, DC: American Psychological Association.

Anderson, J. (2010). *Cognitive Psychology and Its Implications,* 7th Edition Freeman: New York.

Bacon, S. M. (1992a). The Relationship between Gender Comprehension, Processing Strategies, and Cognitive and Affective Response in Foreign Language Listening. *The Modern Language Journal, 76(2)*: 160-178.

Bacon, S. M. (1992b). Authentic listening in Spanish: How learners adjust their strategies to the difficulty of the input. *Hispania, 75,* 398-412.

Baleghizadeh, S., & Rahimi, A. H. (2011). The Relationship among Listening Performance, Metacognitive Strategy Use and Motivation from a Self-determination Theory Perspective. *Theory and Practice in Language Studies, Vol. 1, No. 1,* 61-67.

Berne, J. E. (1993). The effects of text type, assessment task, and target language experience on foreign language learners' performance on listening comprehension tests. (Doctoral dissertation, University of Illinois, 1992). *Dissertation Abstracts International, 53,* 2354A.

Berne, J. E. (2004). Listening Comprehension Strategies: A Review of the Literature. *Foreign Language Annals, Vol.37, No.4,* 521-531.

Boekaerts, M., Pintrich, P., & Zeidner, M. (2000). *Handbook of self-regulation.* San Diego: Academic Press.

Bolitho, R., Carter, R., Hughes, R., Ivanic, R., Masuhara, H., & Tomlinson, B. (2003). Ten questions about language awareness. *ELT Journal,* 57(3), 251–260.

Brown, G. (1977). *Listening to Spoken English.* London: Longman.

Buck, G. (1995). How to Become a Good Teacher. In D. J. Mendelsohn, & J. Rubin (Eds.), *A Guide for the Teaching of Second Language Listening* (pp.13-30). San Diego: Dominie Press.

Buck, G. (2001). *Assessing Listening.* Cambridge: Cambridge University Press.

Caplan, D. (1972). Clause boundaries and recognition latencies for words in sentences. *Perception and Psychophysics, 12,* 73-76.

Carrier, K. A. (2003). Improving High School English Language Learners' Second Language Listening Through Strategy Instruction. *Bilingual Research Journal, 27, 3,* 383-408.

Chamot, A. U. (1987). The Learning Strategies of ESL Students. In A. Wenden & J. Rubin (Eds.), *Learning Strategies in Language Learning* (pp. 71-83). Englewood Cliffs, NJ: Prentice-Hall.

Chamot, A. U. (1995). Learning strategies and listening comprehension. In D. J. Mendelsohn, & J. Rubin (Eds.), *A Guide for the Teaching of Second Language Listening* (pp.13-30). San Diego: Dominie Press.

Chamot, A. U., & Küpper, L. (1989). Learning strategies in foreign language Instruction. *Foreign Language Annals, 22, 1:*13-24.

Chang, A. C-S., & Read, J. (2006). The Effects of Listening Support on the Listening Performance of EFL Learners. *TESON Quarterly, Vol. 40, No.2,* 375-397.

Chang, A. C-S. (2008). Listening Strategies of L2 Learners With Varied Test Tasks. *TESL Canada Journal, Volume 25, Issue 2,* 1-22.

Chang, A. C-S. (2009). EFL Listeners & Task-based Strategies and Their Relationship with Listening Performance. *The Electronic Journal for English as a Second Language, Vol. 13, No.2,* 1-28.

Chao, J. Y. (1997). The influence of strategy use on comprehension and recall of authentic listening texts by Chinese EFL students in Taiwan. (Doctoral dissertation, University of Minnesota, Twin Cities, 1996). *Dissertation Abstracts International, 57,* 3366A.

Chen, Y. (2007). Learning to learn: The impact of strategy training. *ELT Journal, 61(1),* 20-29.

Chien, C-N., & Wei, L. (1998). The Strategy Use in Listening Comprehension for EFL Learners in Taiwan. *RELC Journal, 29,* 66-91.

Conversion Table of Standarised Tests. (n.d.). Retrieved on May 20, 2014, from http://www.eigodejuken.com/level.html

Cross, J. (2009). Effects of listening strategy instruction on news videotext comprehension. *Language Teaching Research, 13,* 151-176.

Cross, J. (2010). Metacognitive instruction for helping less-skilled listeners. *ELT Journal, 65(4),* 1-9.

Cutler, A. (2012). *Native Listening Language Experience and the Recognition of Spoken Words.* England: The MIT Press.

DeFilippis, D. A. (1980). *A Study of the Listening Strategies Used by Skillful and Unskillful College French Students in Aural Comprehension Tasks.*

Unpublished doctoral dissertation, University of Pittsburgh. U.S.*EIKEN* (n.d.) Retrieved on August 10, 2014, from http://www.eiken.or.jp/eiken/en/eiken-tests/

Eilam, B., & Aharon, I. (2003). Students' planning in the process of self-regulated learning. *Contemporary Educational Psychology,* 28, 304–334.

Field, J. (1998). Skills and strategies: Towards a new methodology for listening. *ELT Journal 52/2,* 110-18.

Field, J. (2000). Finding one's way in the fog: listening strategies and second-language learners. *Modern English Teacher, Vol. 9, No.1,* 29-34.

Field, J. (2003). Promoting perception: lexical segmentation in L2 listening. *ELT Journal, 57 (4),* 325-334.

Field, J. (2008). *Listening in the Language Classroom.* Cambridge: Cambridge University Press.

Field, A. (2009). *Discovering statistics using SPSS.* (3rd ed.). London: SAGE.

Flavell, J. H. (1979). Metacognition and cognitive monitoring: a new area of cognitive-developmental inquiry. *American Psycholo*gist, *34/10:* 906-11.

Fujinaga, M. (2002). なぜ英語が聞き取れないのか？- 学生のディクテーションから [Why can't learners listen and comprehend? – An analysis with dictation]. *Keizai Riron, No. 306,* 1-22.

Fujiwara, B. K. (1990). Learner training in listening strategies. *JALT Journal, 12:2,* 203-217.

Gimson, A. (1980). *An Introduction to the Pronunciation of English.* 3rd ed. Hong Kong: Edward Arnold.

Goh, C. (1997). Metacognitive awareness and second language listeners. *ELT Journal, 51 (4),* 361-369.

Goh, C. (1998). How ESL learners with different listening abilities use Comprehension. *Language Teaching Research, 2(2),* 124-147.

Goh, C. (2000). A cognitive perspective on language learners' listening comprehension problems, *SYSTEM, 28,* 55-75.

Goh, C. (2002). Exploring listening comprehension tactics and their Interaction patters. *SYSTEM, 30, 2,* 185-206.

Goh, C. (2008). Metacognitive instruction for second language listening development: theory, practice and research implications. *RELC Journal, 39,* 188-213.

Goss, B. (1982, April). *Listening to Language: An Information Processing Perspective.* Paper presented at the Annual Meeting of the Southern Speech Communication Association, Arkansas, U.S.

Graf, P., & Torrey, J. W. (1966). Perception of phrase structure in written language. *American Psychological Association Convention Proceedings,* 83-88.

Graham, S., & Macaro, E. (2008). Strategy instruction in listening for lower-intermediate learners of French. *Language Learning, 58,* 747-783.

Graham, S., Santos, D., & Vanderplank, L. (2008). Listening comprehension and sstrategy use: a longitudinal exploration. *SYSTEM, 36, 1,* 52-68.

Graham, S., Santos, D., & Vanderplank, L. (2011). Exploring the relationship between listening development and strategy use. *Language Teaching Research, 15(4),* 435-456.

Hamamoto, Y., Harada, Y., Iyoda, Y., & Kamuro, M. (2013). 日本の大学生のリスニング・ストラテジー使用と習熟度の関係 [Correlation between the usage of listening strategies by Japanese university students and their proficiency levels]. *The Japan Association of College English Teachers Kansai Journal, 15,* 40−59.

Henrichsen, L. E. (1984). Sandi-Variation: A Filter of Input for Learners of ESL. *Language Learning, 34,* 103-26.

Ho, H. (2006). *An Investigation of Listening Comprehension Strategies Used Among English-Major College Students in Taiwan – A Case of Chaoyoung University of Technology.* Unpublished master's thesis, Chaoyoung University of Technology, Taiwan.

Hughes, A. (1989). *Testing for language teachers.* Cambridge: Cambridge University Press.

IELTS (n.d.) Retrieved on August 10, 2014, from https:// www.eiken.or.jp/ielts/en/merit/

Ikemura, D. (2003, May). 音声聞き取り困難の克服をめざすリスニング指導：キーワードと文脈の有効利用を考える [Listening instruction for acoustic problems: a consideration of effective usage of keywords and contexts]. Paper presented at spring programme of Kansai Chapter, The Japan Association for Language Education & Technology, Osaka, Japan.

The Institute for International Business Communication. (2013). *TOEIC® Programme Data & Analysis.* Retrieved on October 15, 2013, from http:// www. toeic.or.jp/library/toeic_data/toeic/pdf/data/DAA2012.pdf

Itakura, T., Ohsato, F., & Miyahara, F. (1985). ディクテーション：その理論的背景・評価としての妥当性・誤答の類型 [Dictation: its theoretical background, reliability as an assessment, error patterns]. *Language Laboratory, 22,* 3-25.

References

Ito, H. (1990). Comprehension gap between listening and reading among Japanese learners of English as a foreign language, *Annual Review of English Language Education in Japan, 1,* 13-27.

Jarvella, R. J. (1971). Syntactic processing of connected speech. *Journal of Verbal Learning and Verbal Behavior, 10,* 409-416.

Kakehi, H., Suenobu, M., Young, R., Kanzaki, K., & Yamane, S. (1981). An analysis of perceptual error: Learning process, *JACET Journal, No.12,* 133-144.

Kiriki, K. (2002). *ANOVA4 on the Web.* Retrieved August 10, 2014 from http://www.hju.ac.jp/~kiriki/anova4/

Kline, R. B. (2004). *Beyond significance testing: Reforming data analysis methods in behavioral research.* Washington, DC: American Psychological Association.

Knowles, G. (1987). *Patterns of Spoken English.* Hong Kong: Longman Group, U.K. Limited.

Ladefoged, P. (1982). *A Course in Phonetics.* U.S.: Harcourt Brace Jovanovich, Inc.

Laviosa, F. (1992). *A preliminary investigation of the listening problem-solution process and the strategies of five advanced learners of Italian as a second language.* Unpublished doctoral dissertation. State University of New York, Buffalo.

Liberman, A. M. (1970). The grammars of speech and language. *Cognitive Psychology, 1,* 301-323.

Lynch, T. (1998). Theoretical perspective on listening. *Annual Review of Applied Linguistics, 18,* 3-19.

Lynch, T. (2009). *Teaching Second Language Listening.* Oxford: Oxford University Press.

Lynch, T. & Mendelsohn, D. (2002). Listening. In N. Schmitt (Ed.), *An introduction to applied linguistics* (pp.193-210). London: Arnold.

Mendelsohn, D. J. (1994). *Learning to Listen: A Strategy Based approach for the Second Language Learner.* San Diego: Dominie Press.

Mendelsohn, D. J. (1995). Applying Learning Strategies in the Second/Foreign Language Listening Comprehension Lesson. In D. Mendelsohn, & J. Rubin (Eds.), *A Guide for the Teaching of Second Language Listening* (pp.132-150). San Diego: Dominie Press.

Mizumoto, A. & Takeuchi, O. (2011). 効果量と検定力分析入門 - 統計的検定を正しく使うために[An Introduction about Effect Size and Power

Analysis −For Correct Statistical Analysis]. 『より良い外国語教育研究のための方法』外国語教育メディア学会 (LET) 関西支部 メソドロジー研究部会 2010 年度報告論集 [*Methodology for Better Foreign Language Research − LET Kansai Chapter, Methodology Research Group Report in 2010 Academic Year*], 47-73.

Mokhtari, K., & Reichard, C. (2002). Assessing students' metacognitive awareness of reading strategies. *Journal of Educational Psychology, 94*, 249–259.

Moreira, M. L. (1996). On listening comprehension: Linguistic strategies used by second language learners in non-collaborative discourse. (Doctoral dissertation, University of Illinois at Urbana-Champaign, 1995). *Dissertation Abstracts International, 56*, 3562A.

Morris, S. (1983). Dictation: A technique in need of reappraisal, *ELT Journal, 37(2)*, 121-126.

Murphy, J. (1985, March). *An Investigation into the Listening Strategies of ESL College Students.* Paper presented at the 19th Annual Meeting of the Teachers of English to Speakers of Other Languages, New York, U.S.

Murphy, J. (1987). The Listening Strategies of English as a Second Language College Students. *Research & Teaching in Developmental Education, Volume 4, No.1,* 27-46.

Nagano, K. (1991). *Investigating FL listening comprehension strategies through thinking aloud and retrospection.* Unpublished master's thesis, Sophia University, Tokyo, Japan.

Nation, I. S. P. & Newton, J. (2009). *Teaching ESL/EFL Listening and Speaking.* U.K: Routledge.

Nishino, T. (1992). What Influences Success in Listening Comprehension?, *Language Laboratory (29),* 37-52.

Oller, J. W., Jr. (1971). Dictation as a Device for Testing Foreign-Language Proficiency, *ELT Journal, 25 (3),* 254-259.

O'Malley, J. M. (1987). The Effects of Training in the Use of Learning Strategies on Learning English as a Second Language. In A. Wenden, & J. Rubin, J. (Eds.). *Learner Strategies in Language Learning* (pp.133-43). London: Prentice Hall.

O'Malley, J. M., & Chamot, A, U. (1990). *Learning Strategies in Second Language Acquisition.* Cambridge: Cambridge University Press.

O'Malley, J. M., Chamot, A. U., & Küpper, L. (1989). Listening comprehension strategies in second language acquisition. *Applied Linguistics, 10,* 418-437.

References

Oxford, R. (1990). *Language Learning Strategies: What Every Teacher Should Know.* New York: Newbury House.

Oxford, R. (1993). Research update on teaching L2 listening, *SYSTEM, 21, 2,* 205-211.

Ozeki, N. (2000). *Listening strategy instruction for female EFL college students in Japan.* Tokyo: Macmillan Language House.

Park, G. (1997). Language Learning Strategies and English Proficiency in Korean University Studies. *Foreign Language Annals, 30, No.2,* 211-221.

Palmer, D. J., & Goetz, E. T. (1988). Selection and use of study strategies: The role of the studier's beliefs about self and strategies. In C. E. Weinstein, E. T. Goetz, & P. Alexander (Eds.), *Learning and study strategies: Issues in assessment, instruction, and evaluation* (pp.77–100). Orlando, FL: Academic Press.

Peters, M. (1999). *Les strategies de comprehension auditive chez des eleves du Bain Linguistique en francais langue seconde* [The listening comprehension strategies of students in an intensive French as a Second Language program]. Unpublished doctoral dissertation, University of Ottawa, Ontaria, Canada.

Rees-Miller, J. (1993). A critical appraisal of learner training: Theoretical bases and teaching implications. *TESOL Quarterly, 27,* 679-689.

Richards, J. C. (2005). Second Thoughts on Teaching Listening, *RELC Journal, 36, 1,* 85-92.

Rivers, W. (1984). What practitioners say about listening: Research implications for the Classroom. In R. A. Gilman, & L. M. Moody (Eds.). *Foreign Language Annals, 17/4.* 331-334.

Rost, M. (2002). *Teaching and researching listening.* Harlow: Longman.

Rost, M., & Ross, S. (1991). Learner use of strategies in interaction: Typology and teachability. *Language Learning, 41,* 231–249.

Rost, M., & Ross, S. (1991). Learner use of strategies in interaction: Typology and teachability. *Language Learning, 41,* 231–249.

Rost, M., & Stratton, R. (2001). 完全攻略リスニング25の鉄則 [25 hard-and-fast rules to master listening]. In S. Onoda (Ed.). Tokyo: Longman.

Rost, M., & Wilson. J. J. (2013). *Active Listening.* UK: Pearson Education Ltd.

Rubin, J. (1988). Improving Foreign Language Listening Comprehension. Research Report on Project #017AH70028 Sept. Washington, DC: U.S. Department of Education, International Research and Studies Program.

Rubin, J., & Thompson, I. (1992). *Materials Selection in Strategy Instruction for*

Russian Listening Comprehension. Washington, DC:U.S. Department of Education. (ERIC Document Reproduction Service No. ED 349796)

Rubin, J., & Thompson, I. (1993). *Improving Listening Comprehension in Russian.* Washington, DC: U.S. Department of Education, International Research and Studies Program. (ERIC Document Reproduction Service No. P017A00032)

Rubin, J. (1994). A Review of Second Language Listening Comprehension Research. *The Modern Language Journal Volume, 78, Issue 2,* 199–221.

Rubin, J., Quinn, J., & Enos, J. (1988). *Improving Foreign Language Listening Comprehension.* Washington, DC: U.S. Department of Education, International Research and Studies Program. (ERIC Document Reproduction Service No. 017AH70028)

Rubin, I. J., & Rubin, I. (1995). *Qualitative Interviewing: The Art of Hearing Data,* 2nd Ed. U.S.: Sage Publications, Inc.

Satori, M. (2010). The Effect of Teaching Phonetic Information Through Repeated Practice of Dictation and Reading Aloud in L2 Listening Class, *Language education & technology (47),* 159-180.

Sheerin, S. (1987). Listening comprehension: teaching or testing? *ELT Journal 41/2*: 126-131.

Shirono, H. (2003). 言語学習ストラテジーを織り込んだ指導でリスニング力を伸ばすアクション・リサーチ [Action Research on Language Learning Strategies to Improve Listening Comprehension in English]. Japan: 三重県桑名高等学校セルハイ研究レポート [Mie Prefectural Kuwana Senior High School Super High Research Report].

Schneider, W., & Shiffrin, R. (1977). Controlled and automatic human information processing: I. Detection, search, and attention. *Psychological Review, 84,* 1-66.

Schoonen, R., Hulstijn, J.,&Bossers, B. (1998). Metacognitive and language-specific knowledge in native and foreign language reading comprehension: An empirical study among Dutch students in grades 6, 8 and 10. *Language Learning, 48,* 71–106.

Shiffrin, R., & Schneider, W. (1977). Controlled and automatic processing: II. Perceptual learning, automatic attending, and a general theory. *Psychological Review, 84*, 127-190.

Suenobu, M., Young, R., Kanzaki, K., & Yamane, S. (1982). An analysis of perceptual error: Effect of learning and mechanism of hearing, *JACET Journal, 13,* 83-97.

Suzuki, K. (2009). リスニング・ストラテジー指導による EFL 学習効果 [Will

listening strategy teaching help EFL learners?]. *Dialogue, 8,* 20-37.

TOEFL® (n.d.). Retrieved on May 20, 2014, from http://www.ets.org/ toefl/ ibt/ about?WT.ac=toeflhome_ibtabout2_121127

TOEIC® Worldwide Report 2012. (2013). Retrieved on 30th May 2014 from http://www.toeic.or.jp/library/toeic_data/toeic/pdf/data/Worldwide_2012.pdf

Thompson, I., & Rubin, J. (1996). Can strategy instruction improve listening comprehension? *Foreign Language Annals, 29,* 331-342.

Tudor, I. (1996). *Learner-centredness as Language Education.* Cambridge: Cambridge University Press.

Ueda, I. (2005). リスニングとその指導 [Listening and its instruction]. In S. Kotera, & H. Yoshida, H. (Eds.), 英語教育の基礎知識 - 教科教育法の理論と実践 [Basic Knowledge in English Education-Theory and Practice]. (Chapter 5, pp.91-109). Japan: Taisyukan Shoten.

Ueda, M. (2013). The Effects of Two Different Teaching Methods on EFL Intermediate Listeners. *Osaka University, Journal of Language and Culture, 22,* 69-81.

Ueda, M. (2014). The Effects of Three Different Teaching Methods on EFL Intermediate Listeners. *English Language Research,* University of Birmingham, 1, 45-85.

Vandergrift, L. (1996). Listening strategies of Core French high school students. *Canadian Modern Language Review, 52 (2),* 200-223.

Vandergrift, L. (1997). The comprehension strategies of second language (French) listeners: A descriptive study. *Foreign Language Annals, 30,* 387- 409.

Vandergrift, L. (1998). Successful and less successful listeners in French: what are the strategy differences? *The French Review, 71 (3),* 370–395.

Vandergrift, L. (1999). Facilitating second language listening comprehension: Acquiring Successful Strategies. *ELT Journal, 53, 3,* 168-176.

Vandergrift, L. (2003). Orchestrating Strategy Use: Toward a Model of the Skilled Second Language Listener, *Language Learning, 53, 3,* 463-496.

Vandergrift, L., & Goh, C. (2009). Teaching and testing listening comprehension. In M. H. Long, & C. J. Doughty (Eds), *The Handbook of Language Teaching.* (pp. 395–411). Blackwell Publishing.

Vandergrift, L., Goh, C., Mareschal, C., & Tafaghodtari, M. (2006). The metacognitive awareness listening questionnaire: development and validation, *Language Learning, 56, 3,* 431-62.

Vandergrift, L., & Tafaghodtari, M. H. (2010). Teaching L2 leaners how to listen does make a difference: An empirical study. *Language Learning, 60,* 470-497.

Vann, R.J., & Abraham, R.G. (1990). Strategies of unsuccessful language learners. *TESOL Quarterly, 24, 2,* 177–198.

Victori, M., & Lockhart, W. (1995). Enhancing metacognition in self-directed language learning. *SYSTEM, 23,* 223–234.

Vogely, A. (1995). Perceived strategy use during performance on three authentic listening comprehension tasks. *Modern Language Journal, 79,* 41-56.

Wang, W. Y. (2002). *Effects of gender and proficiency on listening comprehension strategy use by Taiwanese EFL senior high school students - A case from Changhua, Taiwan.* Unpublished master's thesis, National Changhua University of Education, Changhua, Taiwan.

Watanabe, Y. (2009). Effects of Dictation on TOEIC Listening Comprehension Test : Comparison between two different quantity dictation protocols, *Kokusai Junior College Journal, 24,* 139-156.

Wilson, M. (2003). Discovery listening: improving perceptual processing. *ELT Journal, 57, 4,* 335-343.

Winne, P. (1995). Inherent details in self-regulated learning. *Educational Psychologist, 30,* 173–187.

Wu, Y. (1998). What do tests of listening comprehension test? – A retrospection study of EFL test-takers performing a multiple-choice task. *Language Testing, 15, 1,*8621-44.

Yonezaki, H. (2014). Is Dictation Effective at Improving Listening Comprehension of Japanese High School Learners of English?: An Empirical Study Focusing on Those Who Excel at Reading and Grammatical Competence, *The Chubu English Language Education Society, Vol. 43,* 1-8.

Yorio, C. (1992). *The language learner: A consumer with opinions.* Paper presented at TESON International Conference, Hawaii.

Yoshida, K. (2002). これで身につく！[You can master listening with these tips]. *Power Up Listening, 2,* 32-36. Technological University, Singapore.

Zhang, D., & Goh, C. (2006). Strategy Knowledge and Perceived Strategy Use: Singaporean Students' Awareness of Listening and Speaking Strategies. *Language Awareness, Volume 15, 3,* 199-119.

Zimmerman, B. J., & Schunk, D. H. (2001). *Self-regulated learning and academic achievement.* Mahwah, NJ: Erlbaum.

Appendix A

Schedule of Study I

Week	DTG	LSTG	CG
1	TOEIC®		
2	L1: Reduction of and/or L2: Reduction of to/for/of	Content & Function words	Usual lesson
3	L3: Contraction of be verbs L4: Contraction of will	Working memory Note taking	Usual lesson
4	L5: Contraction of have/has L6: Contraction of would	Inference 1	Usual lesson
5	L7: Contraction of had/had better L8: Contraction of not	Inference 2 Redundancy	Usual lesson
6	L9: Reduction of the words which start with h L10: Reduction of them/him	Discourse markers	Usual lesson
7	L11: Reduction of ~ing L12: Reduction of (be) going to/want to/have to	Background knowledge Adjustment of inference	Usual lesson
8	L13: Reduction of be verbs in interrogative sentences L14: Reduction of be verbs in Wh-interrogative sentences	Inference 3	Usual lesson
9	L15: Reduction of don't/doesn't/didn't in declarative sentences L16: Reduction of be Do/Does in interrogative sentences	Vocabulary Visual aids Background knowledge	Usual lesson

10	L17: Reduction of Did
	    in interrogative sentences
	L18: Reduction of do/does
	    in Wh-interrogative sentences
		Scanning 1	Usual lesson

11	L19: Reduction of did
	    in Wh-interrogative sentences
	L20: Reduction of Do/Does/Did
	    in negative questions
		Skimming	Usual lesson

12	L21: Reduction of Have/Has
	    in interrogative sentences
	L22: Reduction of have/has in
	    affirmative sentences
		Listening literacy	Usual lesson

13	L23: Reduction of auxiliary verbs
	    in interrogative sentences
	L24: Reduction of auxiliary verbs +
	    the present/past perfect
	    in affirmative sentences
		Scanning 2	Usual lesson

14	L25: Omission of Do/Does/Did/be verbs in interrogative sentences	Scanning 3	Usual lesson
15	TOEIC®		

Appendix B

Materials for Dictation Training Group

Week 2-1
Lesson 1: and/or のリダクション (Reduction of and/or)

CD を聞いて下線部に入る語句を書きましょう。
(Listen to the CD and complete the blanks.)

1. John and I are in the same class.
2. Come and see me after the class.
3. John and I are going to the same university.
4. Come and see me anytime.
5. To go or to eat in the shop?

6. Peter or John will help you in a moment.
7. He and I are leaving tomorrow.
8. Sit down and fill out this application, please.
9. John or Bill will be in next Monday.
10. Do you know John and Mary?

11. Come over any time after 2 or 3 o'clock.
12. I received a letter and a package for you.
13. Would you be kind enough to buy me a stamp and an envelope on your way home?
14. I will take a train or a bus on that day.

Week 2-2

Lesson 2: to/for/of のリダクション (Reduction of to/for/of)

CD を聞いて下線部に入る語句を書きましょう。
(Listen to the CD and complete the blanks.)

1. I live next to a post office.
2. Thanks for calling.
3. There was a lot of traffic yesterday.
4. I'm going to the library from now on.
5. This room is not for rent.

6. I'm looking for my mug cup.
7. There are a lot of problems.
8. Will you talk to the student after the class?
9. I went to Mexico for a week.

10. He was standing in the back of the yard.
11. I sent an e-mail to Jack.
12. I saw Eleanor in front of the building.
13. She slept over for an hour.
14. Are there any message for me?
15. The machine has been out of order for a week.

Appendix B Materials for Dictation Training Group

Week 3-1

Lesson 3: be 動詞の短縮形 (Contraction of be verbs)

CD を聞いて下線部に入る語句を書きましょう。
(Listen to the CD and complete the blanks.)

1. I'm OK.
2. We're shocked.
3. Who's that gentleman?
4. I'm tried.
5. We're hungry.

6. Who's your brother?
7. Here's my application form.
8. It's really hot today.
9. Where's Eleanor?
10. They're waiting outside.

11. She's studying in England.
12. We're thinking about going on a holiday.
13. Who's at the back door?
14. What's your passport number?
15. There's a first-aid room on the 3rd floor.

Week 3-2

Lesson 4: will の短縮形 (Contraction of will)

CD を聞いて下線部に入る語句を書きましょう。
(Listen to the CD and complete the blanks.)

1. <u>I'll</u> see you on Sunday.
2. <u>They'll</u> leave London at 8:00.
3. <u>It'll</u> be ready by next Monday.
4. <u>I'll</u> be there in a minute.
5. <u>They'll</u> be late.

6. <u>It'll</u> rain this afternoon.
7. <u>He'll</u> help you.
8. <u>There'll</u> be enough food.
9. <u>It'll be</u> finished by 9:00.
10. <u>Mike will</u> send these boxes.

11. <u>It'll</u> be much hotter tomorrow.
12. <u>Mike will</u> probably pay the bill with a credit card.
13. <u>There will</u> be a short interval after the second act.
14. <u>You will</u> find the key on the back shelf in the room.
15. <u>The doctor'll</u> do in a moment.

Appendix B   Materials for Dictation Training Group

Week 4-1

Lesson 5: have/has の短縮形 (Contraction of have/has)

CD を聞いて下線部に入る語句を書きましょう。
(Listen to the CD and complete the blanks.)

1. I've been here before.
2. He's already gone.
3. You've spent all the money.
4. I've been here many times.
5. He's read most of these books.

6. You've seen this firm.
7. That's happened several times.
8. You've been absent since April.
9. They've changed the system.
10. There's been a horrible accident.

11. I've seen her before.
12. They've already gone.
13. Bill's gone to London by now.
14. It's been going on for a month.
15. She's taught French for 10 years.

Week 4-2

Lesson 6: would の短縮形 (Contraction of would)

CD を聞いて下線部に入る語句を書きましょう。
(Listen to the CD and complete the blanks.)

1. <u>I'd</u> like to book a twin room.
2. <u>It'd</u> be better to tell it to her.
3. <u>He'd</u> say it is ridiculous.
4. <u>I'd like</u> some coffee with milk.
5. <u>They'd like</u> to rest now.

6. <u>It'd be better</u> to pay with a credit card.
7. <u>You'd</u> be surprised to see the place.
8. <u>I'd ask him</u> to report that issue.
9. <u>We'd like to</u> change our seats.
10. <u>There'd be enough food</u>.

11. <u>We'd be</u> glad to have you stay with us.
12. <u>I'd offer</u> you some food, but there's not any in the house right now.
13. <u>It'd be</u> nice to get tickets to the concert.
14. <u>She'd love</u> that gift.
15. I think <u>you'd enjoy</u> that film.

Appendix B   Materials for Dictation Training Group

Week 5-1

Lesson 7: had/had better の短縮形 (Contraction of had/had better)

CD を聞いて下線部に入る語句を書きましょう。
 (Listen to the CD and complete the blanks.)

1. She'd finished the lesson before 6:00.
2. We'd done it.
3. I'd better leave right now.
4. She'd already seen the film.
5. We'd left by 12 noon.

6. I'd better be away from this.
7. You'd better start eating now.
8. She'd met the girl before.
9. We'd arrived at the university by 9:00.
10. I'd better call his family right now.

11. I think we'd better leave now.
12. We'd already revised that article, but we did it again.
13. You'd better listen to your mother.
14. I'd already left the office when you arrived.
15. The doctor said that he'd better not to drink alcohol.

Week 5-2

Lesson 8: not の短縮形 (Contraction of not)

CD を聞いて下線部に入る語句を書きましょう。
(Listen to the CD and complete the blanks.)

1. It <u>isn't</u> snowy today.
2. He <u>hasn't</u> finished his dinner.
3. <u>It isn't time</u> to have a break.
4. <u>They weren't here</u> on that day.
5. <u>He hasn't arrived</u> yet.

6. <u>They don't want to</u> join us.
7. <u>They weren't able to come</u> last time.
8. <u>He didn't say</u> so.
9. <u>They wouldn't go</u> to London.
10. <u>He's not</u> in the 7th grade.

11. <u>We're not</u> interested in that business plan.
12. The child <u>won't</u> be quiet.
13. We <u>can't</u> understand why he didn't come.
14. That <u>doesn't</u> make any sense.

Week 6-1

Lesson 9: h で始まる語のリダクション
(Reduction of the words which start with h)

CD を聞いて下線部に入る語句を書きましょう。
(Listen to the CD and complete the blanks.)

1. He'll call her in the morning.
2. I think he's coming this afternoon.
3. Come here anytime you like.
4. I'll call her again tomorrow
5. I think he's waiting rather long.

6. Come here right now.
7. It's her application.
8. Give it to him when you see him next time.
9. Do you know her and her brother?
10. Is this his seat?

11. He hasn't been here since last year.
12. I need to buy a ticket for him.
13. Is that her sister?

Week 6-2
Lesson 10: them/him のリダクション (Reduction of them/him)

CD を聞いて下線部に入る語句を書きましょう。
(Listen to the CD and complete the blanks.)

1. I'll get them tomorrow.
2. Give them a break.
3. I told them a week ago.
4. I told them to stay here.
5. Why don't you write them a letter?

6. I saw him yesterday.
7. Did you ask him if he could make it?
8. Let's check him again.
9. Have they ever met him before?
10. Have him call her.

11. Tell him Eleanor sent you.
12. I'll put them behind the box.
13. Why don't you write him a letter?
14. One of them is more beautiful than the other.

Appendix B　Materials for Dictation Training Group

Week 7-1
Lesson 11: ~ing のリダクション　(Reduction of ~ing)

CD を聞いて下線部に入る語句を書きましょう。
(Listen to the CD and complete the blanks.)

1. I'm going now.
2. What were you doing at that time?
3. He's working on his essay in Applied Linguistics.
4. Where are you going tomorrow?
5. She isn't doing anything now.

6. Is the car being fixed?
7. What are you doing this afternoon?
8. Are you expecting her soon?
9. I'm learning to speak Japanese.
10. He's going to London next week.

11. How is he doing today?
12. Who is living with her now?
13. He is borrowing some books from the library.
14. They are being giving a presentation in the hall.

Week 7-2

Lesson 12: (be) going to/ want to/ have to のリダクション
　　　　　(Reduction of (be) going to/want to/have to)

CD を聞いて下線部に入る語句を書きましょう。
 (Listen to the CD and complete the blanks.)

1. You're going to/gonna see it.
2. I want to/wanna talk to him.
3. Does she have to revise her classmate's essay?
4. I'm going to leave right now.
5. Are you going to stay here tonight?

6. I want to go with Eleanor.
7. Do you have to leave tomorrow?
8. I'm going to stay home on Sunday.
9. I don't want to take a flight to Manchester.
10. We want to leave at 19:00.

11. They are going to move to London.
12. Do you have to go buy it now?
13. Do you want to drink another glass of orange juice?
14. They are not going to/are not gonna come here anymore.

Appendix B Materials for Dictation Training Group

Week 8-1

Lesson 13: 疑問文中の be 動詞のリダクション
(Reduction of be verbs in interrogative sentences)

CD を聞いて下線部に入る語句を書きましょう。
(Listen to the CD and complete the blanks.)

1. <u>Are you</u> sure?
2. <u>Is it</u> good?
3. <u>Was he</u> able to come on Monday?
4. <u>Are you ready</u> to leave?
5. <u>Is it</u> fun?

6. <u>Was he with you</u> at that time?
7. <u>Were they talking</u> about the project?
8. <u>Is it OK</u> if I sit down here?
9. <u>Were there any problems with it</u>?
10. <u>Is it</u> humid outside today?

11. <u>Are they</u> making too much food?
12. <u>Am I</u> in this group or the other one?
13. <u>Was that</u> your plan?
14. <u>Were you</u> also there?

Week 8-2

Lesson 14: Wh-疑問文中の be 動詞のリダクション
(Reduction of be verbs in Wh-interrogative sentences)

CD を聞いて下線部に入る語句を書きましょう。
(Listen to the CD and complete the blanks.)

1. <u>Where are you</u> going tomorrow?
2. <u>When is he</u> arriving?
3. <u>Who were they</u> working for?
4. <u>Where are you staying</u>?
5. <u>Who were they</u> seeing?

6. <u>What was she doing</u> in the room?
7. <u>How are you going to</u> pay the debt?
8. <u>Why were they</u> upset so much?
9. <u>Who was he talking to</u>?
10. <u>What am I</u> supposed to say?

11. <u>When is he</u> picking his daughters up?
12. <u>Where is it</u> delivered?
13. <u>How are</u> those shoes?
14. <u>Why were you</u> crying yesterday?

Appendix B   Materials for Dictation Training Group

Week 9-1

Lesson 15: 平叙文中の don't/doesn't/didn't のリダクション
(Reduction of don't/doesn't/didn't in declarative sentences)

CD を聞いて下線部に入る語句を書きましょう。
(Listen to the CD and complete the blanks.)

1. I don't like spiders.
2. She doesn't live in London anymore.
3. They didn't turn up yesterday?
4. I don't like still water.
5. They don't arrange the wedding.

6. It doesn't cost as much as the other one.
7. She didn't tell me anything.
8. It doesn't take long to finish marking these tests.
9. We don't have enough money.
10. He didn't know what to say.

11. You don't need to feed guilty.
12. This pen doesn't work.
13. I didn't understand the theory at all.
14. The meeting doesn't start until these computers are fixed.
15. I don't have any question.

Week 9-2

Lesson 16: 疑問文中の Do/Does のリダクション
(Reduction of be Do/Does in interrogative sentences)

CD を聞いて下線部に入る語句を書きましょう。
(Listen to the CD and complete the blanks.)

1. <u>Do you</u> like this place?
2. <u>Does she</u> sleep in here?
3. <u>Does it</u> appeal to many people?
4. <u>Do you know</u> this case?
5. <u>Does she have</u> your mobile number?

6. <u>Do we need</u> this?
7. <u>Does she know</u> how to operate this machine?
8. <u>Does it work</u>?
9. <u>Do you</u> really have to leave now?
10. <u>Do we</u> read page 50 or 15?

11. <u>Does she</u> like tea with cream and sugar in it?
12. <u>Does that</u> make any difference?
13. <u>Does he</u> speak any Spanish?

Appendix B　Materials for Dictation Training Group

Week 10-1

Lesson 17: 疑問文中の **Did** のリダクション
　　　　　(Reduction of Did in interrogative sentences)

CD を聞いて下線部に入る語句を書きましょう。
(Listen to the CD and complete the blanks.)

1. <u>Did you</u> have a good time?
2. <u>Did he</u> give a presentation yesterday?
3. <u>Did we</u> book a room?
4. <u>Did you call him</u> yesterday?
5. <u>Did she call you</u> in advance?

6. <u>Did we win</u> the game?
7. <u>Did he pay back</u> the debt?
8. <u>Did you see</u> the film in London?
9. <u>Did he get</u> the job that he wanted?
10. <u>Did we have</u> any assignment?

11. <u>Did we</u> see this candidate?
12. <u>Did you</u> ask him?
13. <u>Did she</u> quit the course?
14. <u>Did he</u> arrive on time?
15. <u>Did they</u> use these tools?

Week 10-2

Lesson 18: Wh-疑問文中の do/does のリダクション
　　　　　(Reduction of do/does in Wh-interrogative sentences)

CD を聞いて下線部に入る語句を書きましょう。
　(Listen to the CD and complete the blanks.)

1. When <u>do we</u> have to bring these application forms?
2. Where <u>does he</u> live?
3. When <u>does it</u> start?
4. <u>Where do I</u> have to put this suitcase?
5. <u>Where does he</u> work?

6. <u>When does it</u> end?
7. <u>What do you want</u> for breakfast?
8. <u>When does it</u> close?
9. <u>What does he do</u> for a living?
10. <u>How do you</u> want your egg?

11. <u>What does she</u> have in the file?
12. <u>Why does it</u> make a difference?
13. <u>Where does he</u> go for swimming?
14. <u>Who do they</u> work with?

Appendix B　Materials for Dictation Training Group

Week 11-1

Lesson 19: Wh-疑問文中の did のリダクション
　　　　　(Reduction of did in Wh-interrogative sentences)

CD を聞いて下線部に入る語句を書きましょう。
(Listen to the CD and complete the blanks.)

1. Where did I have to put those books?
2. What did you do on that day?
3. When did it open?
4. Where did I put my mobile?
5. What did you do last night?

6. When did it happen?
7. Where did you have to go on that rainy day?
8. Why did he miss the bus?
9. How much did that cost?
10. What did you do in that room?

11. Why did it matter?
12. Where did they hear the news?
13. When did I talk to you last time?
14. Who did she give the information to?

Week 11-2
Lesson 20: 否定疑問文中の Do/Does/Did のリダクション
(Reduction of Do/Does/Did in negative questions)

CD を聞いて下線部に入る語句を書きましょう。
(Listen to the CD and complete the blanks.)

1. <u>Don't you</u> agree?
2. <u>Doesn't he</u> like to join us?
3. <u>Didn't it</u> rain yesterday?
4. <u>Don't you want</u> to go home now?
5. <u>Doesn't he live</u> in London anymore?

6. <u>Didn't it rain</u> on Tuesday's night?
7. <u>Don't you think</u> it's time to start?
8. <u>Didn't it clear up</u> in the evening?
9. <u>Doesn't she</u> want to come along?
10. <u>Didn't you</u> bring your drink?

11. <u>Doesn't he</u> remind you of your father?
12. <u>Don't they</u> need to extend the deadline?
13. <u>Didn't it</u> snow a lot last week?

Appendix B   Materials for Dictation Training Group

Week 12-1

Lesson 21: 疑問文中の Have/Has のリダクション
(Reduction of Have/Has in interrogative sentences)

CD を聞いて下線部に入る語句を書きましょう。
(Listen to the CD and complete the blanks.)

1. <u>Have you</u> ever been to London?
2. <u>Has he</u> talked to the doctor?
3. <u>Has it</u> become widely known to everyone?
4. <u>Have you ever been</u> to England?
5. <u>Has it happened</u> before?

6. <u>Have you called</u> the manager yet?
7. <u>Has he ever talked about me</u>?
8. <u>Have you</u> finished your work yet?
9. <u>Has she</u> ever been married?
10. <u>Has it</u> started to snow yet?

11. <u>Has he</u> solved the case?
12. <u>Have there</u> been any messages for him?

Week 12-2

Lesson 22: 肯定文中の have/has のリダクション
(Reduction of have/has in affirmative sentences)

CD を聞いて下線部に入る語句を書きましょう。
(Listen to the CD and complete the blanks.)

1. <u>I have</u> some hobbies.
2. <u>She has</u> a driving licence.
3. <u>We have</u> a lot in common.
4. <u>I have</u> some work to do.
5. <u>She has</u> a good friend.

6. <u>We have a lot</u> to achieve.
7. <u>It has</u> a complicated lock on it.
8. <u>She has</u> a return ticket to London.
9. <u>It has</u> a good view from the window.
10. <u>We have</u> too many things to do.

11. <u>I have</u> a severe headache.
12. <u>She has</u> a good job.
13. <u>He has</u> many good friends in the army.
14. <u>They have</u> a current account at this bank.
15. <u>It has</u> a lot of protestors.

Appendix B Materials for Dictation Training Group

Week 13-1

Lesson 23: 疑問文中の助動詞のリダクション
(Reduction of auxiliary verbs in interrogative sentences)

CDを聞いて下線部に入る語句を書きましょう。
(Listen to the CD and complete the blanks.)

1. <u>Could you</u> help her?
2. <u>Can you</u> make a call to him now?
3. <u>Could you give</u> me a hand?
4. <u>Should we give</u> this to him?
5. <u>Can you give</u> him a hand?

6. <u>Shall we go</u> after 14:00?
7. <u>Would he help us</u> if possible?
8. <u>Can I borrow</u> this calculator?
9. <u>Should I hand in</u> the assignment?
10. What <u>would you</u> do with a million pounds?

11. <u>Shall we</u> leave now?
12. <u>Could he</u> go with us?
13. <u>Can you</u> pick him up tomorrow?
14. <u>Should I</u> bring this file to him tomorrow?

Week 13-2

Lesson 24: 肯定文中の助動詞＋完了形のリダクション
(Reduction of auxiliary verbs + the present/past perfect in affirmative sentences)

CD を聞いて下線部に入る語句を書きましょう。
(Listen to the CD and complete the blanks.)

1. You <u>must have</u> seen this document.
2. We <u>would have</u> made it if we had left much earlier.
3. They <u>will have</u> completed the project by now.
4. <u>He must have gone home</u> already.
5. <u>We would have come</u> if we had been informed well in advance.

6. <u>By 2001, he will have graduated</u> from the university.
7. <u>You shouldn't have done</u> that kind of thing.
8. Somebody <u>must have taken it</u> seriously.
9. The plane <u>might have been delayed</u> because of the bad weather.
10. They really <u>shouldn't have made</u> that sort of mistake.

11. He <u>must have</u> forgotten the meeting.
12. We <u>would have</u> been lost without your navigation.
13. She <u>could have</u> become a doctor but she didn't.
14. The rain <u>will have</u> stopped by now.
15. That <u>couldn't have</u> been the fatal mistake.

Appendix B　Materials for Dictation Training Group

Week 14-1

Lesson 25: 疑問文中の Do/Does/Did/be 動詞の省略
　　　　　　(Omission of Do/Does/Did/be verbs in interrogative sentences)

CD を聞いて下線部に入る語句を書きましょう。
(Listen to the CD and complete the blanks.)

1. You <u>want</u> some coffee?
2. She <u>come</u> here yesterday?
3. She <u>been</u> sick lately?
4. <u>You want some tea</u>?
5. <u>He come to school yesterday</u>?

6. <u>He call you last night</u>?
7. <u>You seen him recently</u>?
8. <u>She been here</u>?
9. <u>You have</u> his mobile number?
10. <u>Did he find</u> her address?

11. <u>He been</u> in Wimbledon for long?
12. <u>There any cheap apartments</u> in Shrewsbury?
13. <u>Is there any food</u> in the kitchen?

Appendix C

Materials for Listening Strategies Training Group

Week 2

- 内容語 (Content words) → 強く読む (stressed)
  名詞・一般動詞・形容詞・副詞・疑問詞・指示代名詞
  nouns, verbs, adjectives, adverbs, interrogatives, demonstrative pronouns
- 機能語 (Function words) → 弱く読む (unstressed)
  助動詞・冠詞・接続詞・前置詞・関係詞・人称代名詞
  auxiliary verbs, articles, conjunctions, prepositions, relative clauses, personal pronouns

---

<Exercise> Listen to the CD and complete the blanks.

1. forensic:
This expression is relating to the scientific methods used for finding out about a crime.

2. orthodontist:
This is a dentist whose job is to help teeth to grow straight when they have not been growing correctly.

3. surgery:
This is a medical treatment in which a surgeon cuts open your body to repair or remove something inside.

4. bruise:
This is a purple or brown mark on your skin that you get because you have fallen, been hit, etc.

5. clot:
This is a thick almost solid mass formed when blood or milk dries.

Appendix C   Materials for Listening Strategies Training Group

Week 3

- 短期記憶容量について （Working memory）
- ノートの取り方（Note-taking）： 記号、省略、数字などを使う。
  (Use marks, abbreviations, numbers, etc.)

---

e.g.) and   → +   No   → ×
　　　 with   → w)   sixty   → 60
　　　 somebody   → s/b   Sunday   → Su
　　　 anybody   → a/b   10 o'clock → 10:00
　　　 everywhere → e/w   students   → ss
　　　 language   → lg   English   → E
　　　 learning   → lrng   international → int'l

Week 4

- 推測能力 (Inference)（＝音声＋文法＋語彙＋背景的知識など）

    (= voice + grammar + vocabulary + background knowledge, etc.)

   音声 (voice): pitch（高さ）＋ tone（口調）

   ＝ 話し手の感情、性別、年齢、状況などが推測できる。

   (= A listener can guess the speaker's feelings, gender, age, situations, etc.)

<Exercise> Listen to the CD and answer the questions.

Questions:
1. Where was Marisa?
2. What was Marisa doing?
3. What happened to the magazine?
4. What did Marisa plan to do about the magazine?
5. How did Marisa make her eye feel better?

Script:
Marisa was lying down looking at a reading magazine. The room was full of steam. Suddenly she got some soap in her eye. She grabbed the towel wildly. Then, she heard a splash. Oh, no! What would she tell her friend? She would have to buy a new one. She rubbed her eye and it soon felt better.

Appendix C   Materials for Listening Strategies Training Group

Week 5

- 推測能力 (Inference) (＝音声＋文法＋語彙＋背景的知識など)

    (＝voice + grammar + vocabulary + background knowledge, etc.)

    文法的知識の活用 (Active usage of grammatical knowledge)

<Exercise 1> Listen to the CD and choose the appropriate words.

1. This expression is ~~use~~/used to show/~~showed~~ that there is/~~are~~ a lot of ~~thing~~/things to see, do or choose from.

<Exercise 2> Listen to the CD and complete the blanks.

2. He was sick last night.

3. I have done it before.

- 語彙 (Vocabulary)：未知（聞こえない/聞き取れない）の語句の対処法
    (How to understand the words that you do not know)
    →とにかく落ち着く。余剰性(Redundancy)(＝繰り返し)がある。
        (Keep calm and keep listening expecting redundancy.)
            e.g.) What *** means? It means that…, in other words, etc.

< Exercise 3> Listen to the CD and complete the blanks.

Today, I'm going to talk about <u>foods</u> and <u>drinks</u> that can be <u>addictive</u> . Well, what does "<u>addictive</u>" mean? Do you know? Well, it means that a person cannot easily stop consuming something.

Week 6

- 談話標識 (Discourse markers)： (=話しの展開が予測できる材料)
  (= They indicate a speaker's attitude to what s/he is saying next.)
  e.g.)　firstly, secondly, finally, and, but, however, No, So, because, since, for, for example, etc.

<Exercise 1>　Listen to the CD and write three discourse markers.
1.　talk about　　　　　　2.　but　　　　　　3.　and

< Exercise 2> Listen to the CD and write three addictive substances and examples.
　1. caffeine　-----　coffee　　　2.　sugar　3.　chocolate
　　　　　　　-----　tea
　　　　　　　-----　colas　-----　Pepsi
　　　　　　　　　　　　-----　Coke

Script:
Good morning, everyone. Today, let's learn about some addictive substances. Firstly, I'm going to introduce caffeine. That's c-a-f-f-e-i-n-e. It's a natural substance that makes people feel excited or more awake. Many studies have proven that it's addictive. Drinks with caffeine are coffee, tea and colas like Pepsi and Coke. So, they all have the risk of addiction. But it doesn't mean you become instantly addicted by drinking a glass of Pepsi or Coke or a cup of tea or coffee. It only happens when you drink many cups or glasses every day.

Ok, let's move on. Next, I'm going to focus on how caffeine affects our bodies and the dangers of a caffeine addiction. Too much caffeine can cause our heart to "race." And we may have difficulty to sleep. Caffeine can also cause our body to lose water. Furthermore, after having consumed a lot of caffeine for a long period, and then try to quit all of a sudden, we might

Appendix C   Materials for Listening Strategies Training Group

suffer headaches and irritation.

Right, let's move on to another example of something addictive. That is Sugar! Surprise, surprise! Yes, sugar! I know! There's sugar in all sorts of foods and drinks. I know. Americans consume an average of 61kg of sugar every year—that's about 1 to 1.4kg a week! Amazing, isn't it? Actually, it's very difficult to spend a day without eating something with sugar in it. A lot of common foods and drinks such as yoghurt, cereal, soft drinks and lots more. Even spaghetti sauce contains sugar!

Now, we know sugar is another addictive substance. Then, what are the risks of a sugar addiction? If you consume a lot of it, you might feel "high" or happy at first. But later, you feel low or unhappy. And consuming a significant amount of sugar can cause obesity. You become fat. Sugar is also bad for your teeth. But, like caffeine, if you consume moderate amount of sugar each day, you don't have to worry about addiction at all.

OK. I've saved the best example for last. That is chocolate! Because it contains sugar and a couple of chemicals that are like caffeine. So all of the consequences of caffeine and sugar I mentioned are true for chocolate, too.

Week 7

- 背景的知識 (既に知っていること)
  (Background knowledge and Adjustment of inference)

<Exercise 1> Listen to the CD and answer the question.
Why did Eleanor rush into her house?

- 推測の修正
  (Adjustment of inference)

< Exercise 2> Listen to the CD and answer the question.
What is Jenny?

①生徒	先生	主任の先生	その他
student	teacher/instructor	chief teacher/instructor	others
②生徒	先生	主任の先生	その他
③生徒	先生	主任の先生	その他
④生徒	先生	主任の先生	その他
⑤生徒	先生	主任の先生	その他

Script of Exercise 1:
Eleanor heard the ice cream van coming down the street.
She remembered her birthday money and rushed into her house.

Script of Exercise 2:
①Jenny was on her way to school.
②She was so much worried about the English lesson.
③She thought she may not be able to control the class again today.
④She thought it was unfair of the instructor to make her supervise the class for a second time.
⑤After all, it was not a normal part of a junior's duties.

Appendix C   Materials for Listening Strategies Training Group

Week 8

- 推測能力：タイトルのもつ影響力＋背景的知識
  (Inference: the effect of a title + background knowledge)

<Exercise> Listen to the CD and write a summary.

<Two titles>
For Group A, A prisoner who plans his escape
For Group B, A wrestler in a tight corner

Script:
Simon slowly got up from the mat, thinking about his escape, he hesitated for a second and thought. Things were not going well. What bothered him most was being held, though the charge against him had been weak. He carefully considered his present situation. Although the lock which held him was rather strong and hard, he thought he could definitely break it.

Week 9
- 語彙＜音声：3回＞　(Vocabulary → The script was read three times.)
- 視覚情報＜音声：1回＞　(Visual aids → The script was read once.)
- 背景的知識＜音声：1回＞
  (Background knowledge → The script was read once.)

<Exercise> Listen to the CD and write a summary.

Script:
An infant who has a septal defect looks purple. Because the blood cannot get rid of enough carbon dioxide through the lungs.

Vocabulary: septal defect, get rid of, carbon dioxide, lungs

Visual aids:

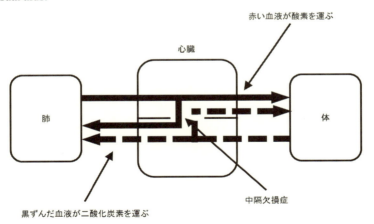

Appendix C Materials for Listening Strategies Training Group

Week 10
- スキャニング 1 (Scanning 1)

<Exercise 1>

You will hear a short conversation between two people. Listen carefully and then read each question and choose the best answer.

1. Where is this conversation taking place?
    (A) In an office
    (B) In an airplane
    (C) At a school office
    (D) On a train platform

2. What did the woman do with the document?
    (A) She sent them to customers.
    (B) She put them in the trash.
    (C) She asked to copy them.
    (D) She read them.

3. How does the man feel?
    (A) Very tired.
    (B) Disappointed.
    (C) Angry.
    (D) Relieved.

Script of Exercise 1:

Man: Do you happen to know where the customer record I gave you yesterday?
          I thought I put them on my desk earlier this morning.
Woman: Oh, I ask Eleanor to copy them. Hasn't she put them back on your desk? I'll check with Eleanor.
Man: Oh, good. I thought you might have discarded them. There is something I need to check before I shred them.

< Exercise 2>

You will hear a short conversation between two people. Listen carefully and then read each question and choose the best answer.

1. What is the topic of the conversation?
    (A) A new TV series.
    (B) Going on a holiday.
    (C) Buying an appliance.
    (D) Selling an old car.

2. What is Argos?
    (A) A television manufacturer.
    (B) A store that sells electronics.
    (C) A TV broadcasting company.
    (D) A large bank.

3. What will the woman probably do in the future?
    (A) Have a big sale.
    (B) Saving enough money.
    (C) Go to Argos.
    (D) Attend a meeting at the bank.

Script of Exercise 2:

Woman: My fridge is too old. I want to buy a large one with a freezer but they're so expensive. I really don't know what to do.

Man: I have an idea. Argos is having a big sale this weekend. Why don't we go and see what they have?

Woman: Good idea. But I don't have enough money. So I need to look for the cheapest one.

Man: I know what you mean. Everything seems to be getting more and more expensive.

Appendix C   Materials for Listening Strategies Training Group

Week 11

● スキミング (Skimming)

<Exercise>

You will hear four statements. Look at the picture and choose the statement that best describes what you see in the picture.

©Masaki Uno

Script:

    A. She may be a nurse.

    B. His tie is striped.

    C. He seems to be upset.

    D. He's wearing a headset.

Week 12

● リスニング・リテラシー (Listening literacy)

<Exercise>

You will hear four statements. Look at the picture and choose the statement that best describes what you see in the picture.

Script:

        A. They are wearing sweaters.

        B. His clothes are formal.

        C. Her basket is full.

        D. She is shopping for clothes.

Appendix C   Materials for Listening Strategies Training Group

Week 13
- スキャニング 2 (Scanning 2)

<Exercise>

You will hear four statements. Look at the picture and choose the statement that best describes what you see in the picture.

1.

2.

Script of 1:

        A. They are wearing sweaters.

        B. His clothes are rather formal.

        C. Her basket is full.

        D. She is shopping for some fruits.

Script of 2:

        A. She's grown up now.

        B. She looks happy.

        C. She seems to be very cold.

        D. She has ice cream on her face.

Week 14
● スキャニング 3 (Scanning 3)

<Exercise 1> Listen to the conversation and choose the best answer for each question.

a. a new exercise tool	d. in a salesroom	g. mother and child
b. helping new colleague	e. in a sport gym	h. salespeople
c. applying for a new job	f. in a TV studio	i. instructor and customer

1. What is the topic of the conversation?   (a.〜c.)
2. Where are they talking?   (d.〜f.)
3. Who are the two speakers?   (g.〜i.)

Script of Exercise 1:

Woman: We're going to start selling a new product here in the salesroom from the next month. I hope it would be very successful.

Man: Oh, really. I didn't know that. What kind product is it?

Woman: Well, it's a new kind of exercise tool that both professionals and non-professionals can use.

Appendix C   Materials for Listening Strategies Training Group

< Exercise 2>

You will hear a short conversation between two people. Listen carefully and then read each question and choose the best answer.

1. What is the man talking about?
    A. Being unsatisfied with a product.
    B. Working at a popular store.
    C. Buying a used television set.
    D. Going back to university as an exchange student.

2. Who might the two speakers be?
    A. Friends.
    B. An attendant and a passenger.
    C. A clerk and a customer.
    D. A teacher and a student.

3. Where might they be speaking?
    A. A travel agency.
    B. A local bank.
    C. A bicycle shop.
    D. An electronics shop.

Script of Exercise 2:

Man: I'm not happy with the iPod I bought here last week. It doesn't seem to have the function that I expected.

Woman: Ok. You can either exchange it for a different one or get your money back.

Man: Umm. I'll have a look at your other products and see if I like anything. Where do you have the ones with higher quality?

Woman: Would you like to come with me? Please come back here when you have made your decision.

< Exercise 3>

You will hear a short conversation between two people. Listen carefully and then read each question and choose the best answer.

1. Where are the people probably speaking?
    A. A school.
    B. A hospital.
    C. A bakery.
    D. A bank

2. What does the man want to do?
    A. Apply for a job.
    B. Withdraw some money.
    C. Set up an account.
    D. Ask about paying rent.

3. Who is the second speaker?
    A. A nurse.
    B. A teacher.
    C. A bank teller.
    D. An accountant.

Script of Exercise 3:

Man: I would like to open a saving account but I don't know what to do. Would you be kind enough to tell me what to do?

Woman: Yes, certainly. Firstly, please fill out this form. Then, sign it and bring it back to me with your bank card.

Man: Sure. I'll be back in a few minutes. May I use your pen?

Woman: There should be a pen at the desk over there.

Appendix D
Raw data of Study I

CG	Wk1	Wk15	D	DTG	Wk1	Wk15	D	LSTG	Wk1	Wk15	D
1	300	325	25	1	275	225	-50	1	295	300	5
2	210	205	-5	2	215	195	-20	2	215	175	-40
3	215	270	55	3	170	220	50	3	295	340	45
4	265	230	-35	4	240	255	15	4	250	235	-15
5	175	205	30	5	215	225	10	5	215	225	10
6	230	230	0	6	225	250	25	6	190	200	10
7	180	160	-20	7	245	265	20	7	230	265	35
8	215	205	-10	8	270	300	30	8	270	265	-5
9	180	205	25	9	260	240	-20	9	280	275	-5
10	175	165	-10	10	205	225	20	10	215	205	-10
Mean	214.50	220.00	5.50	11	220	235	15	11	275	275	0
SD	41.66	48.59	27.33	12	180	195	15	12	285	245	-40
				13	250	310	60	13	250	220	-30
				14	225	275	50	14	250	245	-5
				15	210	210	0	15	185	225	40
				16	190	260	70	16	210	245	35
				17	200	185	-15	17	255	265	10
				18	240	200	-40	18	205	225	20
				19	205	220	15	19	245	205	-40
				20	220	195	-25	20	210	160	-50
				21	215	250	35	21	235	225	-10
				22	275	275	0	22	200	300	100
				23	230	235	5	23	215	265	50
				24	230	290	60	24	230	260	30
				25	185	240	55	25	310	330	20
				26	200	235	35	26	215	290	75
				27	235	300	65	27	260	285	25
				28	260	260	0	28	230	250	20
				29	210	235	25	29	245	250	5
				30	245	280	35	30	275	265	-10
				31	225	270	45	31	245	300	55
				32	260	205	-55	32	200	250	50
				33	235	280	45	33	260	300	40
				34	215	225	10	34	250	315	65
				35	235	315	80	35	195	275	80
				36	205	245	40	36	235	220	-15
				37	215	300	85	37	200	220	20
				38	315	275	-40	38	220	225	5
				39	300	340	40	39	255	295	40
				40	250	245	-5	40	200	285	85
				41	225	295	70	41	235	285	50
				42	255	230	-25	42	300	330	30
				43	260	285	25	43	250	310	60
				44	210	230	20	44	280	385	105
				45	265	305	40	45	265	275	10
				46	230	225	-5	46	270	325	55
				47	195	275	80	Mean	241.30	263.26	21.96
				48	225	270	45	SD	32.41	45.19	37.20
				49	225	315	90				
				50	220	280	60				
				51	245	275	30				
				52	215	210	-5				
				Mean	230.19	253.46	23.27				
				SD	28.90	37.02	35.55				

Appendix E

Schedule of Study II

Week	D+LSTG		CG
1	TOEIC® + MALQ		
2	L1: Reduction of and/or L2: Reduction of and/or	Content & Function words	Usual lesson
3	L3: Contraction of be verbs L4: Contraction of will	Working memory Note taking	Usual lesson
4	L5: Contraction of have/has L6: Contraction of would	Inference 1	Usual lesson
5	L7: Contraction of had/had better L8: Contraction of not	Inference 2 Redundancy	Usual lesson
6	L9: Reduction of the word which starts with h L10: Reduction of them/him	Discourse markers	Usual lesson
7	L11: Reduction of ~ing L12: Reduction of (be) going to/ want to/ have to	Background knowledge Adjustment of inference	Usual lesson
8	L13: Reduction of be verbs in interrogative sentences L14: Reduction of be verbs in Wh-interrogative sentences	Inference 3	Usual lesson
9	L15: Reduction of don't/doesn't/didn't in declarative sentences L16: Reduction of be Do/Does in interrogative sentences	Vocabulary Visual aids	Usual lesson

Appendix E   Schedule of Study II

10	L17: Reduction of Did
	    in interrogative sentences
	L18: Reduction of do/does
	    in Wh-interrogative sentences
		Scanning 1	Usual lesson

11	L19: Reduction of did
	    in Wh-interrogative sentences
	L20: Reduction of Do/Does/Did
	    in negative questions
		Skimming	Usual lesson

12	L21: Reduction of Have/Has
	    in interrogative sentences
	L22: Reduction of have/has
	    in affirmative sentences
		Listening literacy	Usual lesson

13	L23: Reduction of auxiliary verbs
	    in interrogative sentences
	L24: Reduction of auxiliary verbs +
	    the present/past perfect
	    in affirmative sentences
		Scanning 2	Usual lesson

14	L25: Omission of Do/Does/Did/be
	    verbs in interrogative
	    sentences
		Scanning 3	Usual lesson

15	TOEIC® + MALQ		

Appendix F
The MALQ

Strongly disagree	Disagree	Slightly disagree	Partly agree	Agree	Strongly agree
全く違う	反対	どちらかと いうと反対	どちらかと いうと賛成	賛成	全くその通り
1	2	3	4	5	6

1. Before I start to listen, I have a plan in my head for how I am going to listen.
   聞く前に、どのようにして聞くのか頭の中でプランを立てる。   1 2 3 4 5 6

2. I focus harder on the text when I have trouble understanding.   1 2 3 4 5 6
   わからなくなった時は、内容により集中する。

3. I find that listening is more difficult than reading, speaking, or writing in English.
   リーディングやスピーキング、ライティングよりも、リスニングが一番難しい。   1 2 3 4 5 6

4. I translate in my head as I listen. 英語を聞く時は頭の中で訳する。   1 2 3 4 5 6

5. I use the words I understand to guess the meaning of the words I don't understand.
   知っている語彙を使ってわからない語彙を理解しようとする。   1 2 3 4 5 6

6. When my mind wanders, I recover my concentration right away.
   集中力が散漫になったら、すぐにまた集中するようにしている。   1 2 3 4 5 6

7. As I listen, I compare what I understand with what I know about the topic.
   自分が知っている内容と比較しながら聞く。   1 2 3 4 5 6

8. I feel that listening comprehension in English is a challenge for me.
   英語のリスニングは、困難だけれどやりがいがあると感じる。   1 2 3 4 5 6

9. I use my experience and knowledge to help me understand.
   自身の経験や知識を、理解促進のために用いる。   1 2 3 4 5 6

10. Before listening, I think of similar texts that I may have listened to.
    聞く前に、以前聞いたことがある同様の内容を思い出すようにする。   1 2 3 4 5 6

Appendix F   The MALQ

11. I translate key words as I listen.
 重要な語彙は、訳をしながら聞く。
 1 2 3 4 5 6

12. I try to get back on track when I lose concentration.
 集中力がなくなった時は、すぐにまた集中して聞くようにしている。
 1 2 3 4 5 6

13. As I listen, I quickly adjust my interpretation if I realise that it is not correct.
 推測した内容がおかしいなと思ったら、すぐに考えを切り替える。
 1 2 3 4 5 6

14. After listening, I think back to how I listened, and about what I might do differently next time.
 聞いた後に、「どのようにして聞いたのか」「次回はこんな風に聞こう」など、内省する。
 1 2 3 4 5 6

15. I don't feel nervous when I listen to English.
 英語でのリスニングに不安は感じない。
 1 2 3 4 5 6

16. When I have difficulty understanding what I hear, I give up and stop listening.
 聞いていてわからなくなった時は、途中で聞くのを諦めてしまう。
 1 2 3 4 5 6

17. I use the general idea of the text to help me guess the meaning of the words that I don't understand.
 わからない語彙を理解する為に、一般的な知識を用いる。
 1 2 3 4 5 6

18. I translate word by word, as I listen.
 聞く時は、一言一句を訳して聞く。
 1 2 3 4 5 6

19. When I guess the meaning of a word, I think back to everything else that I have heard, to see if my guess makes sense.
 わからない語彙を理解する為に、今迄聞いたことや見たことを用いる。
 1 2 3 4 5 6

20. As I listen, I periodically ask myself if I am satisfied with my level of comprehension.
 リスニングの最中に、定期的に理解できているか自己チェックを入れる。
 1 2 3 4 5 6

21. I have a goal in mind as I listen.
 目的意識を持って聞いている。
 1 2 3 4 5 6

Appendix G

Raw data of Study II

CG	Wk1	Wk15	D
1	230	250	20
2	255	290	35
3	330	365	35
4	310	260	-50
5	210	195	-15
6	250	270	20
7	260	275	15
8	235	315	80
9	275	275	0
10	235	265	30
11	255	240	-15
12	245	230	-15
13	230	260	30
14	190	225	35
15	235	260	25
16	280	275	-5
17	235	240	5
18	205	255	50
19	240	290	50
20	275	290	15
21	250	240	-10
22	230	225	-5
23	250	230	-20
24	205	205	0
25	225	220	-5
26	205	210	5
27	290	340	50
28	280	295	15
Mean	246.96	260.36	13.39
SD	32.58	39.49	27.39

D+LSTG	Wk1	Wk15	D
1	310	270	-40
2	215	280	65
3	310	260	-50
4	250	280	30
5	360	385	25
6	265	270	5
7	275	290	15
8	280	240	-40
9	255	310	55
10	260	280	20
11	300	305	5
12	265	290	25
13	295	325	30
14	235	290	55
15	270	245	-25
16	280	275	-5
17	285	335	50
18	245	270	25
19	255	245	-10
20	220	205	-15
21	305	270	-35
22	230	250	20
23	230	315	85
24	205	210	5
25	230	230	0
26	200	235	35
27	215	270	55
28	220	250	30
29	195	205	10
Mean	257.24	271.90	14.66
SD	39.29	39.94	33.65

Appendix H

Schedule of Study III

Week	DTG	LSTG	CG
1	TOEIC® +	MALQ	
2	L1: Reduction of and/or L2: Reduction of to/for/of	Content & Function words	Usual lesson
3	L3: Contraction of be verbs L4: Contraction of will	Working memory Note taking	Usual lesson
4	L5: Contraction of have/has L6: Contraction of would	Inference 1	Usual lesson
5	L7: Contraction of had/had better L8: Contraction of not	Inference 2 Redundancy	Usual lesson
6	L9: Reduction of the words which start with h L10: Reduction of them/him	Discourse markers	Usual lesson
7	L11: Reduction of ~ing L12: Reduction of (be) going to/ want to/have to	Background knowledge Adjustment of inference	Usual lesson
8	L13: Reduction of be verbs in interrogative sentences L14: Reduction of be verbs in Wh-interrogative sentences	Inference 3	Usual lesson
9	L15: Reduction of don't/doesn't/ didn't in declarative sentences L16: Reduction of be Do/Does in interrogative sentences	Vocabulary Visual aids Background knowledge	Usual lesson

10	L17: Reduction of Did in interrogative sentences L18: Reduction of do/does in Wh-interrogative sentences	Scanning 1	Usual lesson
11	L19: Reduction of did in Wh-interrogative sentences L20: Reduction of Do/Does/Did in negative questions	Skimming	Usual lesson
12	L21: Reduction of Have/Has in interrogative sentences L22: Reduction of have/has in affirmative sentences	Listening literacy	Usual lesson
13	L23: Reduction of auxiliary verbs in interrogative sentences L24: Reduction of auxiliary verbs + the present/past perfect in affirmative sentences	Scanning 2	Usual lesson
14	L25: Omission of Do/Does/Did/be verbs in interrogative sentences	Scanning 3	Usual lesson
15	TOEIC® + MALQ		

Appendix I

Raw data of Study III

CG	Wk1	Wk15	D	DTG	Wk1	Wk15	D	LSTG	Wk1	Wk15	D
1	210	265	55	1	265	335	70	1	275	305	30
2	185	195	10	2	195	225	30	2	295	280	-15
3	200	210	10	3	235	270	35	3	265	280	15
4	170	195	25	4	180	200	20	4	285	325	40
5	185	170	-15	5	195	190	-5	5	245	230	-15
6	195	155	-40	6	195	200	5	6	215	290	75
7	215	240	25	7	180	175	-5	7	245	305	60
8	195	210	15	8	185	205	20	8	240	250	10
9	205	265	60	9	185	245	60	9	220	305	85
10	225	205	-20	10	275	340	65	10	315	285	-30
11	170	190	20	11	230	265	35	11	240	270	30
12	170	175	5	12	255	235	-20	12	280	280	0
13	185	200	15	13	275	320	45	13	275	260	-15
14	190	225	35	14	230	295	65	14	230	245	15
15	280	255	-25	15	255	295	40	15	240	285	45
16	210	190	-20	16	275	255	-20	16	225	285	60
17	235	165	-70	17	295	315	20	17	310	305	-5
18	225	190	-35	18	255	295	40	18	220	250	30
19	180	180	0	19	300	265	-35	19	265	260	-5
20	180	175	-5	20	275	290	15	20	190	225	35
21	230	195	-35	21	260	310	50	21	225	270	45
22	195	195	0	22	270	260	-10	22	225	215	-10
23	230	240	10	23	250	255	5	23	205	260	55
Mean	202.83	203.70	0.87	24	255	340	85	24	195	255	60
SD	26.36	31.20	30.81	25	255	270	15	25	230	235	5
				26	295	285	-10	26	255	235	-20
				27	175	240	65	27	195	220	25
				28	280	285	5	28	255	235	-20
				29	265	320	55	29	285	330	45
				30	260	290	30	30	230	260	30
				31	205	225	20	31	255	200	-55
				32	210	270	60	32	190	245	55
				33	300	360	60	33	225	255	30
				34	210	215	5	34	235	240	5
				Mean	241.91	268.82	26.91	35	240	285	45
				SD	39.16	47.26	30.35	36	255	240	-15
								37	210	275	65
								Mean	242.84	264.19	21.35
								SD	32.22	30.88	33.12